SUPER
BRAIN

SUPER BRAIN

101 Easy Ways to a More Agile Mind

CAROL VORDERMAN
with Theresa Cheung

GOTHAM BOOKS

GOTHAM BOOKS
Published by Penguin Group (USA) Inc.
375 Hudson Street, New York, New York 10014, U.S.A.
Penguin Group (Canada), 90 Eglinton Avenue East, Suite 700, Toronto, Ontario
M4P 2Y3, Canada (a division of Pearson Penguin Canada Inc.); Penguin Books Ltd,
80 Strand, London WC2R 0RL, England; Penguin Ireland, 25 St Stephen's Green,
Dublin 2, Ireland (a division of Penguin Books Ltd); Penguin Group (Australia),
250 Camberwell Road, Camberwell, Victoria 3124, Australia (a division of Pearson
Australia Group Pty Ltd); Penguin Books India Pvt Ltd, 11 Community Centre,
Panchsheel Park, New Delhi–110 017, India; Penguin Group (NZ), 67 Apollo Drive,
Rosedale, North Shore 0745, Auckland, New Zealand (a division of Pearson New
Zealand Ltd); Penguin Books (South Africa) (Pty) Ltd, 24 Sturdee Avenue, Rosebank,
Johannesburg 2196, South Africa

Penguin Books Ltd, Registered Offices: 80 Strand, London WC2R 0RL, England

First published in Great Britain in 2007 by Vermilion.

Published by Gotham Books, a division of Penguin Group (USA) Inc.

First printing, January 2008
10 9 8 7 6 5 4 3 2 1

Copyright © 2007 by Carole Vorderman

Gotham Books and the skyscraper logo are trademarks of Penguin Group (USA) Inc.

LIBRARY OF CONGRESS CATALOGING-IN-PUBLICATION DATA HAS BEEN APPLIED FOR.

ISBN 978-1-592-40345-5

Printed in the United States of America
Set in Galliard
Designed by seagulls.net

While the author has made every effort to provide accurate telephone numbers and
Internet addresses at the time of publication, neither the publisher nor the author
assumes any responsibility for errors, or for changes that occur after publication.
Further, the publisher does not have any control over and does not assume any
responsibility for author or third-party Web sites or their content.

For the three people who most allowed my brain to flourish:

My wonderful and funny primary school headmaster,
Mr. Fred Jemmett, who loved all the children in his care.

My secondary school headmaster, Mr. Frank Ashworth,
who allowed me to come to his school when I was just 10, a year
before the officials wanted. Thank you Sir.

My Mathematics teacher Mr. Parry, who was the best teacher in the
world and for whom I have the utmost respect. Thank you for many,
many happy hours and for teaching us the fourth R—Rigor.

CONTENTS

Acknowledgments   viii

Foreword   ix

Introduction: Strengthen the "Muscle" in Your Head   xvi

Part One: Bionic Brain—101 Exercises for Your Brain

Section One: Concentration   4

Section Two: Memory   28

Section Three: Problem Solving   54

Section Four: Communication   76

Section Five: Creativity   94

Section Six: Reaction Time   108

Section Seven: Mind Power   120

Part Two: Brain Basics—Seven Steps to a Better Brain

Step One: Food for Thought   170

Step Two: Memory Marvels   184

Step Three: The Mozart Effect   192

Step Four: Deep into Sleep   198

Step Five: Let's Get Physical   206

Step Six: Pay Attention Please   212

Step Seven: Use It or Lose It   216

Answers   222

Acknowledgments

Thank you to all the staff at Vermilion who have been so enthusiastic about this book, especially my editor, Julia Kellaway, and Mrs. Boss Lady Clare Hulton. After all our work with colleagues in Ebury Press on the Sudoku books, I didn't think we'd be able to match the pleasure involved, but we have. Thanks, girls.

Thank you to my manager and best friend, John Miles, whose brain power is phenomenal but whose wisdom is even greater.

My biggest thanks go to Theresa Cheung, who has devoted many hours to researching this book. Thank you so much. You've made it a joy.

FOREWORD

"If you don't use it, you lose it." I've heard my mother say that countless times and, much as I rolled my eyes and smirked at the time, as the years have gone on I now see just how true it is. It's worth adding that as far as your brain is concerned, even if you haven't used it for ages and you feel as if you've already lost "it," it's not too late; you can get it back.

The reason you can get it back is because your brain is a stupendous living thing. It is able to repair itself and create new pathways of thought and memory. The power of *your* mind must never be underestimated. *Your* brain needs looking after.

Over the last 25 years, since I started solving the number puzzles on the U.K. Channel 4 TV program *Countdown*, people have talked to me about numbers, and most have been fearful or negative about them (no arithmetical pun intended). For readers who have never seen it, *Countdown* has become a cult show in Britain and is one of the most successful game shows of all time. Some rounds involve contestants being faced with challenging word puzzles and other rounds test mental arithmetic skills. Unlike most other game shows, *Countdown* is all about skill and brain power and the winner gets a teapot—there is no money involved at all! "I can't do sums," "Ooh, I hate math," "Why on earth did we have to learn algebra?". . . and so on. I must have heard just about every opinion about math known to mankind. And yet in Britain and the United States in 2005 Sudoku, the amazing logic puzzle using the digits from 1 to 9, took over the country. People went crazy for it. Couples sat up in bed poring over numbers for hours, waking up in the middle of the night trying to complete their dastardly Sudoku. Millions of books were sold and newspapers found a surge in readership as they produced special pullouts and puzzle pages devoted entirely to Sudoku. When I was in the States promoting Sudoku, I was amazed at how U.S. attitudes to numbers exactly reflected the ones we have in Britain—largely one of fear about math. But Sudoku seemed to transcend all that and people on the subway and buses were happily doing their math puzzles just as much as regular crossworders. It was great to talk to so many Americans about the puzzles and to teach quite a few of them the tricks of the trade through the TV. Even newsreaders who came on strong with their "oh I hate math" attitude (just the same back home in Britain) were convinced of how math can be fantastic by the end of the session. I love all that. I've been fascinated how this puzzle has changed many perceptions about numbers.

Although strictly speaking Sudoku is about logic and not arithmetic, it does activate the same part of the brain that deals with mathematical structures and, because of this, there has been a reawakening of interest and a lessening of fear about numbers. It's an example of how "using it," or rather using a particular part of your brain that perhaps you haven't been using before, gives you a boost to do more and to look at other opportunities using that same part of your brain.

A consequence of the Sudoku phenomenon has been a heightening of interest in the power of the brain—not just in being able to complete a very specific task, such as solving Sudoku, but also how your brain can be retrained so that your thought processes become clearer, more creative, and raise your energy levels in everything you do. I'm a firm believer that the more you use your brain (and your body to some other degree) the more likely you are to achieve happiness.

Age is a strange thing. Every day in the media someone's age is used as a label to imply all sorts of things about them. I hate all this stuff. "He's in his seventies" implies he might not be up to the job. "She's getting on a bit at sixty-three" suggests that this woman is way past her sell-by date and should know better than to think there's plenty of life yet to live. "She doesn't look bad considering she's forty-something"—well, we all know what that means. And yet we all know people who are in their seventies who are far more sprightly than some of those 20 years younger. I've met men and women over 100 years old who appear 30 or 40 years younger than their birth certificates say they are. I know many people in middle age who have more energy than youngsters in their twenties.

I'll never forget getting up at 4 A.M. one morning to get a flight up to Manchester to record *Better Homes*, a hit home renovation and property show in Britain. When I arrived at the airport at the other end at about 7 A.M. one of the members of the production team, a young man of twenty-two, was supposed to be picking me up to drive me to Halifax. Unfortunately, his directions got mixed up and via mobile phone we realized he was completely lost, so I told him to park the car and tell me which street he was on. I then got a cab to his car, got in, and drove him to the location in Halifax. As soon as I arrived I was busy filming, but by 10:30 A.M. our poor driver was so tired he had to go lie down back at the hotel. Meanwhile, the rest of us kept on filming until 9 P.M. when we finished the job. You had to laugh—he was in the bloom of youth and the oldies were wearing him out!

And so it is in life: It is often an attitude of mind that determines whether you will do something or not, as opposed to whether or not you are physically capable of it. Look at the champions of every sport in the world. At the very top they all have similar talents, but what makes a champion is not necessarily what happens with their body, but what happens in their head. Sports psychologists train their heads to make them believe that they can win; it's a crucial part of their training. Well, we can all be champions, not with gold medals swinging around our necks but with victories, large and small, in our lives, every day. And the difference between small successes and a plethora of failures lies in our brains and how we use them.

That's why, when I was asked to put this book together, I didn't want an "exercise book" as such, but something that had a multitude of ideas that you could use without any previous academic study or training. Some of the exercises are so simple I even ask you to sit in a different chair or move your furniture around in your living room at home. It may sound a little silly, but it isn't; it's changing your perspective, and sometimes just a tiny little thing like that can make all the difference. When I first discussed this with my family, being logical creatures they thought I'd gone a bit cuckoo. But it's true. We've made over 4,000 programs of *Countdown* where I stand at the letters and number boards, but whenever I would sit with my cohost Richard Whiteley at his end of the studio and look back at my part of the studio, the whole show appeared so different in my mind. It isn't a view I'm used to at all and it seems bizarre but true.

The most successful products and companies in the world have been born of a simple idea that has looked at an industry from a slightly different perspective. Take the plethora of cheap flight airlines—the simple idea of boarding without a seat allocation makes it faster so that the planes are in the air for more hours every day, making the whole process more economical for the airline and therefore for us. Look at the astonishing success of Google, the world's biggest search engine. Two boys in a backyard with the simplest idea—just type in a word and press "Search"—instead of having to go through the fancy advertising-related pages of other more corporate search engines offering you services you're not interested in. There were many airlines before, and there were many other search engines, but the success has come from seeing the same need from a slightly different perspective.

I really love this book. It's different from my Sudoku books published last year, which were extremely practical with explanations of how to solve the puzzles, together with hundreds of Sudokus to complete. I loved those books with a passion, too, and they sold millions of copies worldwide. But this book is different. I've split it into two parts. The first part has 101 different ways to exercise separate parts of your brain. Some involve logic puzzles or exercises with words, but others may appear less structured. It's vital that you try exercises from each section—from memory or creativity to logic. My natural enjoyment comes from problems involving logic, so I find the other exercises more difficult. However, I have found that they give me more satisfaction and release parts of my brain power that had been lying dormant for years. I want you to give all of the sections a try and see if you can log how you feel your brain is improving. It's always beneficial to make a few little notes—jot them down on the page if that helps you—and then by looking back you'll see what new events and opportunities you're experiencing.

As an example of how important these notes can be, I want to tell you about the hundreds of marvelous people who've written in to *Countdown* to tell us specifically about operations they've had to remove brain tumors and how our TV show has helped. Often the hospitals have organized sessions where the patients are told to watch *Countdown* every day for a month before their operation. In this way, they know on average how good they are at the numbers game, maybe reaching the target 80 percent of the time, and how long their word solutions are, say 6- or 7-letter words. After the operation and during recovery they are asked to watch *Countdown* regularly again. At first their score will be much lower, let's say typically it has reduced from 7-letter word solutions to 3 letters, but as the brain rebuilds its inner pathways, the patient finds that they can eventually return to the 7-letter solutions they used to achieve before the tumor was removed. Hospitals and individuals now see this as a great way of monitoring brain recovery. If those patients can do it, then so can you. A little bit of specific brain exercise every day is all you need.

In the second part of this book I've shown the other ways in which you can help your brain and therefore yourself. Your brain, for instance, needs feeding well. Just as we all know the detrimental effects of alcohol and the devastating effects of drug taking (cannabis often leads to schizophrenia in young adults), we are now more aware of the positive effects certain oils and supplements can have on the speed of activity within your brain. All of this is covered in Part Two. Feed the brain kindly and it will be kind in return.

Don't go away thinking that this is a book for older people. It most certainly is not. This book is suitable for anyone from teenagers to 100-year-olds. We can all improve our brains (me included). I'd like you to start by swapping a 15-minute habit with 15 minutes of brain training every day. You'll soon see the pleasures that come with brain training are far more important than wasting another 15 minutes reading a magazine about celebrities you're never going to meet, or smoking a cigarette. Invest in yourself with 15 minutes a day and you'll see how your opportunities and your happiness increase. Have a good one.

Introduction
STRENGTHEN THE "MUSCLE" IN YOUR HEAD

t doesn't matter how clever you are, how old you are, or how many qualifications you have, you can still increase your brain power. Improving and expanding your mind doesn't have to mean going crazy studying or becoming a reclusive bookworm. There are lots of tricks, techniques, and habits, as well as changes to your lifestyle, diet, and behavior, that can help you flex your gray matter muscles and get the best out of your brain cells. And this book is packed with them!

Your amazing brain

In childhood and the early years of our adult lives we have information pumped into our brain whether we like it or not and then . . . nothing. After formal education and work-related training the brain is left to get on with it and is largely ignored. For much of our lives our brains operate as if on autopilot, thinking and reacting in the same way, even if this isn't getting us what we want.

This book can change all that. It shows you how you can boost your intelligence and improve the quality of your life by giving your brain a workout. To understand exactly how you can boost your brain power, it is useful to understand how the brain works.

Brain wave power

The brain is composed of billions of nerve cells or neurons. They "talk" to each other with electrical signals and brain chemicals called neurotransmitters. The electrical signals travel along branch lines known as axons and dendrites. A single long axon sprouts from each neuron and then divides into numerous branches. These axon branches link up with the dendrites of other neurons. A neuron has lots of dendrites—so many they look like a bottle brush!—making up nine-tenths of the brain cell's surface area.

Connections between axons and dendrites are called synapses and act like "on" or "off" switches. When an electrical signal reaches the end of an axon, a neurotransmitter is released into the synapse, and this triggers (or blocks, if it's an "off" switch) a signal in the dendrite it's

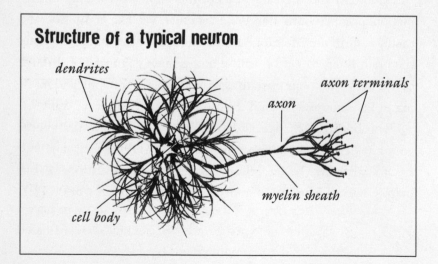

Structure of a typical neuron

dendrites

axon terminals

axon

myelin sheath

cell body

attached to. If a neuron gets enough "on" signals from its neighbors it fires off its own signal. In this way, waves of signals pulsate through the brain thousands of times a minute, controlling movement and processing data.

Every time you stimulate your brain, a unique network of connections is activated. If you have acquired a new skill or learned a new piece of information, this creates yet more connections in your brain, and also strengthens the ones you already have.

The more you use your brain, the better it gets. This applies to anyone, regardless of age or circumstances. For example, the brain of a dyslexic person differs from that of a normal reader, but this does not mean that the dyslexic person's brain is inferior or can't be changed— quite the contrary. It actually can often be very creative and can develop and change, just like any other brain.

It was once thought that brain power decreased with age, but research has shown this simply isn't true. Your brain remains highly adaptable, able to acquire new skills and information well into old age. So you can increase your knowledge, intelligence, and abilities at any stage in life. The huge growth in Sudoku puzzles proves that. A year or two ago most people in Britain and the United States had never tried Sudoku (including me!). Now it has a huge following, with enthusiasts of all ages eager to get their daily Sudoku fix! Not only are more people playing Sudoku, but it has encouraged many more to have a go at different types of puzzles, including word-based puzzles they'd never attempted before.

How powerful is the human brain?

If you're still unsure whether your brain is up to the task, think about the huge potential locked up inside your head. The brain's power is truly awesome. It has been calculated that the brain contains 100 billion neurons. That number—a 1 followed by 11 zeroes—is more than all the stars in the Milky Way.

But that pales into insignificance compared with the potential number of connections between neurons, and the number of brain patterns they could form. It is estimated that this number could be as high as 1 followed by 800 zeroes! That's more than all the atoms in the universe! When you think of all the skills, knowledge, and memories that could be stored in those brain patterns, the genius of Mozart, who composed his first music at the age of five, seems, well, child's play! That gives you an idea of what your mind can achieve— a *super* brain indeed. So there's no reason why you can't make use of that potential to sharpen your own mind skills.

Brain studies

With the development of new brain scanning systems, such as magnetic resonance imaging (MRI) and positron emission tomography (PET), we can almost "see" the brain in operation. These scanners show which parts of the brain become active—appearing to light up—as you think or do certain things. The diagram opposite shows

Brain map

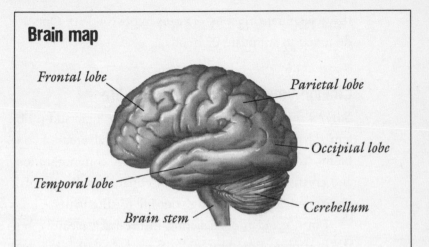

Frontal lobe

Parietal lobe

Occipital lobe

Temporal lobe

Cerebellum

Brain stem

Parietal lobe: Concentration and problem solving.
Frontal lobe: Problem solving, communication, and creativity.
Occipital lobe and cerebellum: Reactions and motor skills.
Temporal lobe: Language, memory, creativity,
and communication.
Brain stem: Involuntary functions, such as
heart and breathing rate.

The "left" hemisphere, which influences problem solving, logic, and reasoning and controls the right hand.

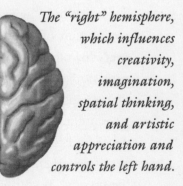

The "right" hemisphere, which influences creativity, imagination, spatial thinking, and artistic appreciation and controls the left hand.

the main brain regions. The exercises in Part One are designed to stimulate them all.

Change your brain, change your life

Super Brain is not just about developing logic and problem-solving abilities but about improving all areas of your brain—concentration, memory, reactions, communication, and creativity. In short, it's about enhancing all aspects of your mind and so changing your life for the better.

I'm not old (no snickering in the back please!), but the pressures of modern life—particularly with a business to run and a family to look after—do take their toll. It's very easy, particularly for women, to feel as though our brains are weighed down with a thousand things to remember. Lists are my solution to this. If I can put notes onto paper I don't have to carry that bit of information in my head anymore. I still have to do the job, but it frees up a lot of space in my brain for other more immediate tasks and worries, and pleasures, too.

If you're in high school or college studying for exams, the amount of knowledge you have to take in can seem overwhelming. *Super Brain* helps you get to grips with your studies and recall *what* you need *when* you need it. Or perhaps you feel you're getting forgetful with age. It's a common worry. Memory problems can sap your confidence and self-esteem. The techniques in this book will help strengthen your memory and boost self-esteem in the process. If you find it hard to concentrate for more than a few minutes, it can affect your performance at school or work, especially when learning new skills. Again, there are tips in this book to help you focus and tackle any subject with ease.

Do you long to write a novel or start your own business but simply can't come up with the right ideas? Maybe you struggle to find the words that express how you really feel? Whatever your age or situation, *Super Brain* is designed to open and expand your mind, boost your confidence, and add a sparkle to everything you think and do. Use it to change your mind and your life for the better. There are tips and techniques here that can help you achieve your goals.

A whole brain workout

After centuries of research, not only do we know that the brain can change and adapt, we also know that it is a two-part organ. The right side of the brain mainly controls the left side of the body and the left brain mainly controls the right side of the body.

In most people, the left side of the brain is the logical, rational side. It deals with facts, diagrams, dates, letters, numbers, math skills, language, point-by-point information, and shaping ideas. Timing and rhythm, necessary for developing music-playing skills, are here, too. The right side deals with color, imagery, perspective, spatial relationships, and other complex visual patterns. Imagination, intuition, and insightful thinking are located here, along with the ability to recognize and remember tones, melodies, sound quality, and intensity—needed for musical

What's Your Brain Type?

Do you watch the clock constantly, or wait until the rumble of your stomach reminds you it's time to take a break? Do people say you are "down to earth" or "up in the clouds"? These characteristics are associated with your brain type. Typically, dominant left-brainers are meticulous, precise, organized, and think things through practically and logically. They feel happier when they have guidelines, rules, and schedules to follow. On the other hand, right-brainers are dreamers. They are often more spontaneous, imaginative, and intuitive than cautious left-brainers and tend to follow their gut feelings.

Most of us are neither strongly logical nor strongly intuitive but somewhere in between—and that's perfectly normal. Everyone is different and has characteristics of both types. Though right-brain thinking is often regarded as more "creative" than left-brain thinking, there is no right or wrong here. They are merely two different forms of thought process. One is not better than the other, just as being right-handed is not "superior" to being left-handed.

What's important is to stretch your mind by trying out different ways of thinking. Whatever your natural preference, your brain will be stimulated by these exercises. If you are strongly practical and logical (left brain), pay particular attention to the creativity, communication, and memory exercises. If you are strongly intuitive and creative (right brain), the concentration, problem-solving, and reaction sections are especially significant for you.

appreciation. The right brain recognizes faces. The left brain recognizes names. Only when both sides are fully involved in learning can we reach our full potential.

Part One: Bionic Brain presents 101 savvy brain teasers and exercises to flex your "mental muscles" and strengthen your mind. Some exercises work your left brain—the rational, logical part of your mind—while others work your right brain—the intuitive, creative, imaginative part. Together they give you a well-rounded brain workout and equip you to meet any mental challenge—whether it's remembering a name or where you put your mobile phone, being creative in your work, holding your own in any conversation, or mastering a new skill.

How to get the best out of this book

To use this book in the most effective way, have a go at all the sections in *Super Brain*. Don't just stay within your comfort zone. For example, if you're good at logic, you may find yourself automatically turning to the problem-solving sections first. However, the creativity exercises would probably be better for you in helping to develop the more neglected areas of your brain.

Before you begin, take a moment to answer the questions on the following page, as they can help you discover your strengths and weaknesses. They can also give you guidance on the best places to start and help identify which sections in Part One will challenge your brain. Try a couple every day for a month and see how you do.

❑ Are you good at crosswords or Sudoku? If you are, try the creativity exercises.

❑ Do you always remember birthdays and anniversaries? If so, challenge yourself with the communication exercises.

❑ Are you the life and soul of the party? If that is the case, have a go at the concentration exercises.

❑ Have you always thought of yourself as artistic and creative? If you have, tackle the problem-solving exercises.

❑ Can you shut out distractions easily? If you can, try the reaction time exercises.

❑ Is it easy for you to unwind at the end of the day? If so, you might want to challenge yourself with the memory exercises.

❑ Are you a creature of habit? Then you need to do some mind power exercises.

Part Two: Brain Basics—Seven Steps to a Better Brain is an important supplement to the exercises in Part One. It explains how simple changes to your lifestyle and behavior can help keep you mentally fit. You'll also learn what the latest research has uncovered about your brain's ability to develop and how simple steps such as healthy eating, regular exercise, and the right kind of mental stimulation can all boost your brain power.

Have fun exercising your brain

The exercises in this book are designed to be enjoyable as well as mentally stimulating, so have fun as you tackle them. Feel free to flip through this book, selecting and working with any exercise that grabs your attention. However you decide to work with the book, remember that mental fitness—your ability to concentrate, reason, imagine, solve problems, and be creative—depends on how well and how often you challenge and exercise your brain.

To recap, the brain has the capacity to keep changing and developing throughout life, so you can boost your intelligence and knowledge at any age. Loss of brain power isn't inevitable with age and intelligence is not fixed at birth. Most age-related losses in memory and mental ability simply result from inactivity and lack of mental exercise and stimulation. In other words, use it or lose it.

Reading and working through this book could be the best and most important decision you ever make. It will limber up your mind and power up your brain circuits. You may even find that it sparks new interests, hidden talents, ideas, and confidence you didn't know you had.

I hope you enjoy the mental exercise and stimulation *Super Brain* offers!

Bionic Brain
101 Exercises
for Your Brain

t his is your brain fitness center. It is designed to give your "mental muscles" a good workout. You choose how you use this section according to what you want to achieve. You can work through the whole section from start to finish, or concentrate on those sections that interest you—it is entirely up to you. For some of the exercises you'll need a way to time yourself. A kitchen timer—or any timer with an alarm—is ideal, since it alerts you when the time is up without your needing to keep checking a watch or a clock.

Take care not to overdo it. Mental exercise can exhaust you without you realizing it. If you get a headache, stop and take a break. Work at your own pace and build up your mental strength and stamina as you go along. These exercises are enormously powerful, and you may feel some of the brain-boosting benefits instantly as your brain becomes more alive. If practiced regularly, these exercises could have a dramatic effect on your brain power—and your life!

You may want to dip into Section Seven: Mind Power right away, as it is packed with simple exercises that will boost brain function and are fun to do. You can do them anytime, anywhere, whenever you have a spare moment. Or you may prefer to tackle the more detailed challenges for Concentration (Section One), Memory (Section Two), Problem Solving (Section Three), Communication (Section Four), Creativity (Section Five), and Reaction Time (Section Six) first.

When you've finished, check your answers in the back of the book—but don't cheat! Give all the exercises a try first. You'll be surprised what you can achieve if you stick with it. So put on your thinking cap, get started, impress your friends and family, and have some fun at the same time.

Section 1
CONCENTRATION

Concentration is good brain exercise. Brain scan images show that there are immediate increases in blood flow whenever the mind is stimulated. This stimulation encourages the growth, density, and efficiency of the all-important axons and dendrites, the dense tree-like branches that link the brain cells (see page xviii).

A focused mind is a powerful mind. Improving your ability to concentrate helps you avoid the problems, disappointments, and misunderstandings that occur when you can't keep your mind on the job. In short, better concentration makes your life easier. This section deals with breathing exercises, deep relaxation, concentration, and visualization. It will help you focus better, improve your existing mental powers, and discover others you didn't even know you had!

Before you start, check your powers of concentration as they are at the moment. If you answer "yes" to more than 3 of the following 10 questions, you should pay special attention to this section.

❑ Are you easily distracted from the task at hand?
❑ Do you find it hard to play games that demand intense concentration, such as chess?

❑ Do you find it hard to unwind at the end of the day?

❑ Does your mind often wander?

❑ Do you often miss deadlines?

❑ Do you prefer doing rather than thinking?

❑ Do you find studying or working from home particularly hard?

❑ Do you spend more than two hours a day watching television?

❑ Does your brain often feel "foggy," as though you can't think clearly?

❑ Do you find it hard to spend time on your own?

To get maximum benefit from the following exercises, choose a time when you are unlikely to be disturbed. For example, you could do them when the rest of the family is out of the house and you have some time on your own. Then switch on the answering machine, switch off your mobile phone—and relax!

1 Focus on Your Breath

Aim: To help you improve your mental focus using a simple breathing technique.

Focusing on the breath is one of the most widely used and effective techniques to aid meditation.

Task: Close your eyes and breathe deeply and regularly, as follows. Inhale through your nose slowly and deeply, feeling your lower chest and abdomen inflate like a balloon. Hold for five seconds. Exhale deeply, deflating your lower chest and abdomen like a balloon. Hold for five seconds. Focus your full mind on your breath as it flows in and out of your body. Give your full attention to the breath as it comes in, and full attention to the breath as it goes out. Whenever you find your attention wandering away from your breath, gently pull it back to the rising and falling of your chest. Do this for about five minutes and then allow your breathing to return to its normal rhythm.

2 Change Your Mood

Aim: To use simple distraction techniques to alter your emotional state.

Your thoughts and feelings, just like your intelligence, are not set in stone. You have the power to change them. Negative thoughts, worries, and fears can often interfere with concentration, but it is possible to change the way you feel. Just as it is possible to enhance your mind using simple techniques, so can you counter negative emotions, too.

Task: The next time you are feeling low, take a shower, change your clothes, or tidy up your office. Go for a brisk walk or dance to music. If you're at home, vacuum the living room, open a window, or change the sheets. As you do these simple activities, imagine that your worries are written down on separate sheets of paper. Mentally pick up each sheet, rip it up, and throw it away. Change your focus to all that is good about your life. Think about what makes your life great.

If you found this exercise helpful, use it every day to ensure that you always "get out of bed on the right side." First thing in the morning, lie in bed or sit in a comfortable position and concentrate on the positive mood you want to create for the day ahead.

If it didn't work for you, perhaps you just need to *let yourself be* for a while. For example, if you've experienced a loss of some kind, you may need to have a good, long cry. If you feel frustrated or angry, you might need to rant and rave to get it out of your system. The important point is to let yourself *feel it*—even if it really hurts. A bad attitude is usually the result of suppressed feelings, and those feelings will interfere with your concentration until you can find ways to release them.

3 Figment of Your Imagination

Aim: To improve your ability to focus by means of simple visualization techniques.

Task 1: Sit comfortably, close your eyes, and imagine as vividly as you can a cup of tea, coffee, or hot chocolate set on a table in front of you. Now reach out your hand and imagine picking it up. It's a large cup, the kind you get in coffee shops, with a matching saucer. Imagine feeling the hardness of the cup, the weight as you lift it up, and how it pulls down on your fingers. Imagine bringing the cup to your lips and "see" how it looks as it moves and tilts toward you. Did you feel like having a cup of tea after you did this?

If you managed this exercise without any difficulty, try this one. It looks simple, but unless you stay completely focused you won't be able to do it.

Task 2: Take an actual fruit (an apple, for example) and really study it. Concentrate all your attention on it and examine it from all directions. Devote the whole session to concentrating on it. Do not be carried away by any irrelevant thoughts that may arise. Stay with the fruit. Just look at it, see it, smell it, and touch it, and don't think about anything else.

Helpful hint: To be successful at visualization you need to pay attention to details and incorporate all your senses—smell, sound, taste, and touch, as well as sight.

You might like to try the following technique, too. It will require all your powers of observation.

Task 3: Choose any book, open it at random, and count the words in a single paragraph. Count them again to be sure that you have counted them correctly. Start with just the one paragraph and, when that task becomes easy, count the words on a whole page. Perform the counting mentally and only with your eyes, without pointing your finger at each word. This sounds easy, but it requires your full attention and all your powers of concentration. Have a go and find out!

If you found this exercise difficult, you may have more success with the next one.

4 Know Your ABCs

Aim: To test your knowledge of the alphabet and enhance your powers of concentration at the same time.

Task: Pick out individual letters from the rows of letters shown below, according to the following rules. In the first line, pick out letters that are next to each other in the alphabet. For example, AB, FG, ST.

In the second line, pick out letters that have two letters between them in the alphabet. For example, AD, FI, TW.

In the third line, pick out letters that have three letters between them in the alphabet. For example BF, MQ, RV.

You can use the same letter twice. You've got three minutes. How many pairs of letters can you get?

P B D R S U W I G K L J O Q S F N L
C E H K I J H R T V P M J H N A Q
F J T X B D K O R T O S W A E I

(Answer on page 223.)

> *Helpful hint:* Try
> writing out the alphabet
> before you begin, as it is
> tough trying to do this
> in your head.

If you found around 15 pairs in total, you're doing well. Keep trying to find the other pairs. You'll find this exercise helps you get a lot more out of crossword puzzles and word search puzzles. If you haven't done a crossword puzzle before, don't jump straight in with the *New York Times* crossword. Start with something easy and gradually build up to higher levels.

If you found fewer than 10 pairs in total, it is worthwhile putting in a little more practice. It will really help your powers of concentration. But this time, before you begin, still your mind with some of the meditation exercises shown earlier and see if you can improve your score.

5 Watching the Clock

Aim: To enhance your ability to keep your mind completely focused by concentrating on one thing.

Task: Take an analog clock (one with a second or "sweep" hand) and put it in front of you so you can clearly read it. Wait until the second hand arrives at 12. Now focus all your thoughts on the movement of that second hand. If one thought interferes with your concentration, stop the exercise and wait until the hand is at 12 and then start again. Aim to focus on the second hand for just five seconds at first and slowly increase.

Once you can do this exercise for a few seconds, try to build up to 30 seconds. If you are distracted by restless thoughts, count the seconds in your mind as you follow the hand. With practice, you should arrive at the point where your mind is totally focused on the moving hand and nothing else.

> *Helpful hint: Before trying this, it may help to do the deep-breathing exercise to calm your mind. Do the Watching the Clock exercise every day, little by little, until you improve. You'll find it gets easier with practice.*

6 Mantra—Just Say "Om"!

Aim: To enhance your powers of concentration using classical meditation.

Whether spoken or not, words and sounds create vibrations that can be used in meditation.

Task 1: Close your eyes and breathe deeply and regularly. Focus on a word or phrase that has meaning to you. It could be a mantra, a name, a relaxing sound such as "Om," or a concept that has special power or significance for you. Repeat the word in your mind with each exhalation. If your mind wanders, gently return it to focus on the word as you repeat it with each breath.

If you managed this exercise okay and got through the five minutes without falling asleep or getting fidgety, well done! Keep practicing every day and don't increase your time until you start to really enjoy those five minutes. Once you find it all a piece of cake, increase your time to 15 or 20 minutes.

If you found it difficult to concentrate or sit still, try shortening the time you spend on this to just a few minutes. Don't give up,

> *Helpful hint: If you find yourself getting bored and fidgety in this exercise, it means you are not focusing your entire mind on what you are doing. Try to blot out all other thoughts. One useful technique is to count each in-breath up to 10 and then count each out-breath back down to 1 again. Meditation takes time and effort to do well, so if you want to be good at it, you need to persist and practice daily.*

though, as those who have most difficulty concentrating often get the most out of this exercise once they learn how to do it well.

If you find that you easily become distracted, have a go at the following techniques:

Task 2: Whenever you notice your mind starting to wander away from whatever you are trying to focus on, simply say to yourself: "Be here now," and gently bring your attention back to where you want it to be. If your mind wanders again, repeat "Be here now," and bring your attention back. Don't be cross with yourself or try to force yourself to concentrate.

When you are *thinking* about not concentrating, you are *not concentrating*! Don't try to push any particular thought out of your mind. When you are trying *not to think* about something, your mind is occupied with that and—again—you are *not concentrating*. Just let the thought go, like a balloon in a breeze. Say to yourself, "Be here now," and return to the present.

Task 3: When you find that something is distracting you or bothering you in any way, make a conscious decision to "let it be." Try not to let the situation irritate you. Do not wish it to change. Just allow it to be. This technique is good for everyday situations that you have to live with, such as noisy children, cooking smells, the sound of next door's television, the humming of your computer, and really distracting noises, such as drilling or traffic. It might help to combine this with the previous techniques. Take a deep breath and breathe out slowly. As you breathe out, let go of any tension or irritation you might have. Say to yourself, "Be here now," and bring your attention back to where you want it to be.

Task 4: Set aside worry or daydreaming time. If your mind is regularly side-tracked into worrying or daydreaming during the day, set aside a specific time each day, say 6 P.M. to 6:30 P.M., to think about whatever it is that keeps interrupting your concentration. Research has shown that people who regularly use a worry time worry less. So set a specific time each day to do your worrying. Almost any time will do—but not just before you go to bed. During the day, when your concentration is distracted by thoughts or worries, tell yourself to put it out of your mind until your "special time," when you'll think about it. Let the thought go. Use the "Be here now" technique, if you like. Be sure that you keep the promise with yourself and do your worrying when the time comes! Stop when the time is up, and continue the next day. You can use the same technique for daydreaming. Don't stop daydreaming altogether, though, as experts believe it can benefit your brain and your creativity. Just daydream at times when you don't need to concentrate on something or someone else!

7 Relaxation and Concentration

Aim: To boost your powers of concentration through relaxation techniques.

You may think that relaxation is the opposite of concentration, but in order to stay focused for long periods it is absolutely vital that you take time out to recharge your batteries. Relaxation thoroughly refreshes your mind, reduces stress and anxiety, and helps you focus on the task at hand. Below you'll find one short and one long relaxation technique that you may wish to use anytime during your day, while studying, before a presentation or speech, prior to a big date or an interview, or whenever.

Task 1: Short Relaxation. Loosen any tight clothing and get comfortable.

Tighten the muscles in your toes. Hold for a count of 10.

Now relax, and enjoy the sensation of release from tension.

Flex the muscles in your feet. Hold for a count of 10. Relax.

Move slowly up through your body—legs, abdomen, back, neck, face—contracting and relaxing your muscles as you go.

Breathe deeply and slowly.

Task 2: Long Relaxation. Remove yourself from all noise and interruption. Find a comfortable position, such as sitting in a soft chair or lying on a bed. Make sure that your head, upper back, and neck are supported. For the next 20 minutes, focus on yourself and let your mind and muscles rest.

Now close your eyes and focus on your breathing. Breathe slowly and deliberately. Give all your attention to your breath coming in and going out. As you inhale and exhale, focus on your body relaxing and release stress and pain.

Now that you are breathing slowly and relaxing your body, think of a pleasant place. Perhaps you are on a sandy beach, dozing as you lie on soft white sand under a warm sun. Use all your senses as you imagine this lovely place: See the clear ocean, feel the warmth of the sun and the mild breezes. Take as long as you need to savor the peace of the location you have created in your mind!

Helpful hint: If you have difficulty focusing and your mind wanders during this task, don't give up! But don't force yourself to complete the task; just try again another time. Relaxation techniques work best when you do them regularly, preferably at the same time of day. Make it a habit and you'll reap the benefits.

As you imagine your perfect place, consider your body. Are there any areas that feel tight or tense? Concentrate on those areas and imagine the tension slipping away. Feel the warmth of the relaxation start to replace the tension. Feel free to move slowly to help this process.

At the end of your deep relaxation period, take a

few deep breaths and slowly open your eyes. Stay in the same position for several minutes before moving on to something else.

If this worked for you, why not try it just before you go to sleep tonight? You may find that your sleep is deeper and more relaxing than ever before.

If you found it hard to unwind, try to slow things down even more when you do this exercise and really take your time.

8

Turn the Volume Down

Aim: To enhance your hearing in order to improve your concentration.

Task 1: Turn on the television or radio and lower the volume until you can barely hear what is being said. Then slowly turn up the volume until you can hear clearly what is being said. Make a note of when you hit that point with the volume indicator on your screen or radio. Repeat this exercise several times a day and try to hit that point earlier each time. Every time you try the exercise, work to hear the talking more clearly and sooner than last time.

> *Helpful hint: This exercise works best with radio, rather than TV, as there are no images to distract you. Your ears get used to a certain volume, but often that volume is far higher than you need to hear clearly. Use a talk station rather than a music one.*

Task 2: Fine-tune your hearing with a little music if the volume indicator on your television or radio didn't drop much in the previous task. It might help to play a piece of music that you enjoy and, while you are listening, draw a picture of what you hear. The picture does not have to be realistic. It could be abstract shapes or colors that express the ideas or feelings that come to you as you listen. You might also want to try the following meditation technique to sharpen your hearing.

Task 3: Close your eyes, breathe deeply and regularly, and separate yourself from the chatter of the stream of thoughts that flow through your mind. As your mind quiets and you relax, become aware of the variety of sounds that surround you. There is no need to do anything but listen. If this worked for you, why not put your amazing listening skills to good use and practice on friends and family, as follows?

Task 4: Over the next few days, make a point of really listening to your friends, family, and colleagues and pay attention to what they say. Try to keep your interruptions to a minimum, and just listen. You'll be surprised at what you learn and how much other people appreciate being heard.

If you found it hard to unwind in order to do any of the tasks in this exercise, try to slow things down even more when you do this exercise and really take your time. It may help to prepare by doing some of the meditation exercises beforehand.

9 Mind Wandering

Aim: To use unfocused thoughts to discover how your mind operates.

Task: Get comfortable and relax. Take deep breaths for a few minutes and just stay quiet. Your mind will begin to wander, but don't try to stop it. Just let it go wherever it wants to go and watch it as if you were a spectator. Don't try deliberately to have positive thoughts or push away unpleasant ones. After a while you'll notice how fickle your thoughts are, how they spring up in your mind and then slip away. If you can do this for about 10 minutes, you will begin to learn interesting things about your mind.

Helpful hint: The key is to practice. In time it will become easier and easier to impose silence on your thoughts.

You will find out which thoughts try to dominate and which ones are quickly pushed aside.

If you managed to do this for about five minutes, you are doing well. To improve your concentration skills, keep practicing and try to extend to 10 minutes, then 15, and then 20 and really find out what makes you tick.

If you didn't like this exercise, or found it difficult, consider why you are uncomfortable with your thoughts. Is there something troubling you? If there is, it will interfere with your concentration until you can find ways to deal with it.

10 Candle Magic

Aim: To improve your powers of concentration using a simple focusing technique.

Task: Light a candle and place it on an empty desk or table in front of you. Now stare at the candle for 10 seconds, then close your eyes and imagine every detail of the candle. Think about the candle's shape and color and how the flame flickers. Try to keep this image in your mind for as long as possible. You might find this hard at first and may need to open your eyes again to refresh your memory and try again. Practice for a few minutes each day until you have mastered the skill and, for safety reasons, be sure to snuff out your candle completely when you have finished.

If this technique worked for you, keep practicing slowly and steadily and aim to build up to 10 minutes a day. Once you've done that, try a mandala meditation. A mandala, like the one below, is a design that represents

the universe and is used by mystics to focus and inspire the mind during meditation. Follow the same instructions, but this time working with the mandala instead of a candle.

Meditating on a candle or mandala is the kind of exercise you can return to again and again so, if you found it difficult this time, try some of the other exercises in this section and come back to this exercise later.

Helpful hint: This kind of exercise really takes time to learn and do well, so be patient. Practice slowly and steadily over a period of several weeks and you will find it gets easier.

11 Getting Down to It

Aim: To enhance your powers of concentration in everyday tasks.

Task: The previous exercises have relaxed and prepared you. Now it's time to put them to the test in your daily life. Choose a job that you need to do today—it could be anything, housework, making a phone call, whatever—and give it your undivided attention for 30 minutes. That may not seem like a long time, but you need to work steadily and resist the temptation to daydream or to think about anything else.

Helpful hint: The best way to succeed at this task is to create an environment that helps you concentrate. Some people like music and chatter, but others need peace and quiet. Find what works best for you. Take regular breaks and you'll find this will refresh and reenergize your mind and your mood.

If you managed to concentrate for 15 minutes, well done! Keep practicing and soon you'll be able to go for 30 minutes. If you get to the magic 30 minutes, you have an iron concentration. Congratulations!

If your concentration kept wandering, try again but this time for a shorter period, say 10 or 15 minutes, and work your way up to 30 minutes.

Measure your progress so far

Set a timer for three minutes. Put on some pleasant music and, using the hand that you don't usually write with, draw a sideways figure 8 in the air. Do this figure 8 air drawing over and over again, making the figure a little larger and larger until it is huge, then start making it smaller and smaller again. When it is very small, make it larger again, and so on. Repeat for three minutes.

If you were able to do this for at least two of the three minutes without your mind wandering, you're making steady progress and really improving your powers of concentration. This is a great exercise to do whenever you feel you need to improve your concentration, as it activates both eyes and stimulates both sides of your brain. Note: This exercise can be done without movement, simply by imagining drawing the different-size figures.

Section 2
MEMORY

the act of memorizing encourages the brain cells to lay down more connections, creating new neural networks in which the newly acquired memories are stored. Many people believe they have a poor memory because they cannot recall names, faces, dates, and so on. Often the problem is not that memories have been lost but that you are out of practice when it comes to retrieving the memories that you *have* stored.

Memory is like a muscle and the more you use it the stronger and fitter it will get. So, the more information you memorize, the easier it becomes to recall stored information. Although poor diet, poor health, and stress can adversely affect it, by getting into the habit of flexing your "mental muscle," your memory gets regularly refreshed and strengthened and grows fitter and sharper than ever.

Before you start, check the state of your memory at the moment. If you answer "yes" to more than 3 of the following 10 questions, you should pay special attention to this section:

❑ Do you find it hard to put names to faces?
❑ Do you get embarrassed when you need to introduce people because you have forgotten their names?

❏ Do you forget appointments or tasks, even when you've written them down in your date book?

❏ Do you often get lost?

❏ Do you often forget where you have put personal items, like your car keys or your mobile phone?

❏ Do you sometimes forget where you parked your car or bike?

❏ Do you often forget special events such as birthdays and anniversaries?

❏ Do you sometimes enter a room and forget why you went in there?

❏ Do you sometimes forget what you were about to say?

❏ Do people often say to you "You've already told me that"?

12 Kim's Game

Aim: To flex your "memory muscle" and power up your observational skills.

This game is derived from Rudyard Kipling's novel *Kim*. In the novel, the game was used to train the young hero, Kim, and other students in the skills required to carry out clandestine operations in colonial India.

Task 1: Look at the illustrations below for one minute and try to memorize all the items. Then close this book and write a list of everything you can remember.

> *Helpful hint: With this kind of observational task it helps to remember the objects visually (as one picture) rather than trying to recall them individually by name. Close your eyes and try to visualize the objects exactly as they are in the illustration. Just look at your mental image and check off each object as you see it. When you do this you are using "working memory." This is the short-term storage facility you use to carry out tasks such as looking up a restaurant telephone number in a directory and holding it in your mind long enough to dial it.*

If you remembered fewer than six of the objects, your memory is out of condition—but don't worry about it, you're in the majority! Most of us need to fine-tune our memory. If you practice this kind of exercise again and again you'll soon notice an improvement.

Task 2: Ask someone to collect 12 different items for you. Observe them for one minute and then try to recall as many as you can. It might help to connect the items together by making up some kind of story that includes them all. When you do this you are involving both hemispheres and more areas of the brain, and this can really help your recall.

If you remembered at least eight of the items, you are doing well. Try the exercise again, but this time try to remember them all. You could ask someone to collect different items for you, but this time introduce more objects—up to 16. Here is another one to try:

Task 3: Find a picture in a book, magazine, or newspaper that is full of objects. Study the picture for a minute and then try to remember 12 or more items—people, animals, buildings, or whatever—illustrated in the picture.

In Kipling's novel, the eponymous hero practiced this skill until he was expert. If you want to improve your memory, you can be as good as Kim with constant practice.

If you managed to remember 11 or more of the items, you're ready for a really tough version of the game using 24 objects. Score over 20 and you'd make a great spy!

13

Memory Rituals

Aim: To use ritual techniques to jog your memory.

Task 1: Have you ever tied a knot in a hanky to remind you to do something important? If you have, then you are using ritual to boost your memory. For this task, think of something you need to remember to do— such as write a thank you note or pick up items from the dry cleaners—and then think of a ritual you can use to assist your memory. For instance, you could put a chair in front of the steps to remind you to take out the garbage, or leave a single piece of fruit in the middle of the kitchen table to remind you to pay the bills.

Helpful hint: In order to work effectively, the ritual needs to be bizarre or unusual enough to make an impression on your unconscious mind and so prompt your memory at the appropriate time. You could tie a pink ribbon around a door handle, or put a familiar object, such as a photograph, paperweight, or picture, on your desk in a different position so every time you look at it and notice the unusual position your memory is jogged.

If this task worked for you, keep practicing and try the following one.

Task 2: On a day when it isn't important that you be somewhere on time in the morning—such as while you're on vacation—ditch the alarm clock and program your body clock to get up at a certain time using a ritual. For example, before you go to bed, repeat five times out loud the time you want to wake up while doing something unusual such as gentle stretching from side to side. You'll be surprised at how well this self-waking technique works, but note that this technique needs practice and may not work the first time for everyone.

If you practiced a ritual but still forgot what you needed to do, perhaps your ritual wasn't striking or unusual enough. Try again with something really unusual.

14 The Book Club

Aim: To test your memory and your powers of observation.

Task 1: Study the picture for five minutes, then turn the page and try to answer the questions. The picture is of a seating plan. It shows the names of 10 members of a book club positioned around a square table, and lists each member's favorite author.

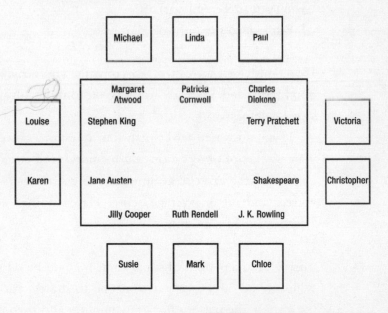

Helpful hint: It helps to memorize the table one side at a time. Try to visualize the names and the authors.

❑ How many men were present?

❑ Who is Susie's favorite author?

❑ Who sat opposite Karen?

❑ Who sat to the right of Christopher?

❑ Who sat on the left of the person who read Jilly Cooper?

❑ Who was the favorite author of the person who sat opposite Paul?

❑ Who sat to the left of Louise?

❑ Who read J. K. Rowling?

❑ Who read Terry Pratchett?

❑ Who sat to the right of Mark?

If you answered at least seven correctly, you achieved a good result and are ready to move on to more advanced visual memory work.

If you answered fewer than four questions correctly, your powers of observation and memory need strengthening. Try the exercise again until you get at least seven correct and hit an average score. Have another go at Exercise 12: Kim's Game.

Task 2: Find a pattern of some kind. It could be on your wallpaper or carpet, or get someone to draw a pattern. Now study the pattern for a few minutes and then draw it, first with your right hand and then with your left hand. Next, try to draw it from memory. This is a test of visual memory, not artistic skill, so don't worry if your drawing isn't up to speed. The idea here is to remember as many details as you can of the pattern.

Association

Aim: To use association techniques to boost memory.

Association is an extremely useful technique for remembering important details such as phone numbers and addresses.

Task 1: Find familiar words, images, or phrases and associate them with some information you are trying to commit to memory, such as an important name and telephone number you came across recently. The association does not have to make logical sense. In fact, it is often those associations that are particularly odd, humorous, or silly that stay in your mind. Some people remember names this way. For instance, you may remember the name Robert Green by picturing Robert playing golf (on the green), wearing green clothes, or covered in green paint. Telephone numbers can become silly jingles; for example, 423–622–4001 becomes: Four to three. Six tutu. Four oh oh, one.

Now that you are familiar with the technique, use it to help you with the next task.

Task 2: Memorize the fictional names, addresses, and phone numbers below. Study them for five minutes and then use your powers of association to remember them.

**Graham Warren, 44 Barley Street,
New York, NY 10007–1201**

**Rebecca Cartwright, 4606 Park Heights Avenue,
Baltimore, MD 21215–6332**

Michael Paine, 101 Cherry Street,
Seattle, Washington, 98104–2205

Raymond Carmichael, 8262 South Shore Drive,
Chicago, IL 60617–2151

The more ridiculous your associations the more likely you are to remember them. Does Rebecca do her cartwheels right? Can gray ham (Graham) be eaten with barley? The more bizarre and exaggerated you make the associations, the better this technique works. It might also help to add rhymes and songs as well.

If you find you can work with this technique, you have mastered a memory tool that can be of enormous help to you. See if you can still remember the addresses tomorrow, and then in a week's time. Use this technique to memorize all your important phone numbers and addresses.

Do you remember how you learned your ABCs? Try this task.

> *Helpful hint: Here's a basic memory rule—you can remember any new piece of information if it is associated with something you already know or remember. Is there anyone you know who has the same first name or last name? Does the name of the street conjure any familiar images?*

Task 3: Make a list of 4 to 6 errands you need to do in the next day or so. Then pick a tune you like and set your list to music. You'll be amazed at how this enhances your memory.

16

Repeat After Me!

Aim: To use repetition as a memory aid.

Task 1: Repeat the following poem out loud several times and then try to repeat it with your eyes shut. If you already know the poem by heart, find one you don't know. Give yourself 10 minutes for this task.

The Road Not Taken (1915)

Two roads diverged in a yellow wood,
And sorry I could not travel both
And be one traveler, long I stood
And looked down one as far as I could
To where it bent in the undergrowth.

Then took the other, as just as fair,
And having perhaps the better claim,
Because it was grassy and wanted wear;
Though as for that, the passing there
Had worn them really about the same.

And both that morning equally lay
In leaves no step had trodden black.
Oh, I kept the first for another day!
Yet knowing how way leads on to way,
I doubted if I should ever come back.

I shall be telling this with a sigh
Somewhere ages and ages hence:
Two roads diverged in a wood, and I—
I took the one less traveled by,
And that has made all the difference.
Robert Frost

Helpful hint: Try to learn the poem in sections. Memorize the first three lines. Then add the next three lines and so on. Repetition is the key. Repeat. Repeat. Repeat. Work on memorizing it for several minutes. Leave it and then come back to it and repeat again and again. It will come!

It might help to take a break and come back to it in an hour or so. You may find that the break recharges your memory. If you still find it hard to remember the poem, it might help to try the next task:

Task 2: Get a sheet of paper and copy out the Robert Frost poem. Underline the important words in it. Decide on a tune and sing the words to it. Read them aloud. Now put them aside and write as much as you can remember. You may amaze yourself by how well you do.

If you could do this exercise after only a few repetitions and within 10 minutes, you have a fantastic tool for memory work that can benefit you enormously in your daily life. Now try this:

Task 3: Choose a new poem, wise saying, Bible verse, or meaningful statement from a book, magazine, or newspaper and memorize it. Repeat the exercise every day. Your brain loves this kind of stimulation.

17 I Know Who You Are!

Aim: To link names with faces by means of a simple observational technique.

Task 1: Look at the 10 names and faces below for two minutes. Then cover up the names with a sheet of paper. Go away and do something else for half an hour, then come back and try to identify the names just by looking at the people.

John

Natalie

Janet

Elizabeth

Harry

Maurice

Teri

Sam

Tom

Mary

Helpful hint: One way to remember people is by distinctiveness. Home in on a particular feature, the shape of the forehead, the hairstyle, how far apart the eyes are. It is often more difficult to remember the names of children, as their features are more rounded and less distinctive than an adult's. In everyday life it can help you to remember names if you place the person in context and try to remember where you have seen him or her before.

If you got most of the names and faces right, use your gift to win friends and influence people.

If you could only remember up to four names and faces, try again and look for particular qualities, or any associations you can make. If you can't find any, make them up. Does anyone look happy or sad, kind or unkind, or remind you of someone you know? What about hair-style or expression? Try giving them imaginary characters or lifestyles. Now try this task:

Task 2: The next time you are introduced to someone new, don't only remember their name but find out a few personal facts about them and see if you can recall these details the next time you meet. You'll end up seeming cleverer and being more popular than you already are.

18

Can't Get You Out of My Head!

Aim: To use music to fine-tune your memory.

Task 1: Set some information you need to remember to a favorite piece of music or a well-known catchy song. For example, have a go at setting the signs of the zodiac in their correct order to "Happy Birthday" or "The Star-Spangled Banner" or the children's nursery rhyme "Jack and Jill":

Aries

Taurus

Gemini

Cancer

Leo

Virgo

Libra

Scorpio

Sagittarius

Capricorn

Aquarius

Pisces

> *Helpful hint: Choose a really simple tune. Children's nursery rhymes are ideal. Don't worry if the tune doesn't fit particularly well, because this will make it even more memorable. The parts that don't scan are likely to be the ones you remember best.*

If you already know the zodiac, choose something you don't know, such as the brightest stars in the sky or the 12 cranial nerves.

Once you get the hang of it, with practice, try this harder challenge.

Task 2: Learn the major bones in the human body: skull, maxilla, mandible (man-di-bl), vertebrae, clavicle, scapula, humerus, ribs, wrist, carpal, metacarpal, phalanges (fa-lan-jez), radius, ulna, pelvis, sacrum, femur, patella, tibia, fibula, tarsals, and metatarsals. Alternatively, choose an uplifting poem, speech, or passage about 20 lines or so long from a book you love. Set it to music and let the beautiful words sink into your memory.

If you find this exercise hard work, try the repetition task again from Exercise 16. You might find the next exercise, Mnemonics, will help you too, and you might also find it useful to read about "The Mozart Effect" in Part 2 (see page 192).

19

Mnemonics

Aim: To use the technique of mnemonics to help you remember useful information.

Mnemonics is a useful technique that helps jog your memory. For example, the following mnemonics are sentences or phrases in which the initial letters of the words spell out words that many people find rather tricky to spell.

A R I T H M E T I C
A Rat In The House May Eat The Ice Cream

N E C E S S A R Y
Not Every Cat Eats Sardines (Some Are Really Yummy)

B E C A U S E
Big Elephants Can Always Understand Small Elephants

Here is another example, a word list, showing the order in which the planets orbit the Sun in our solar system:

Sun, Mercury, Venus, Earth, Mars, Jupiter,
Saturn, Uranus, Neptune, Pluto:

Shirley McLaine Vomits Every Morning,
Jimmy Stewart Usually Never Pukes

OR My Very Excellent Mother Just Showed
Us Nine Planets

Task 1: Listed below are 15 commonly misspelled words, so create a mnemonic that helps you spell them correctly.

MINUSCULE

MILLENNIUM

EMBARRASSMENT

OCCURRENCE

ACCOMMODATE

PERSEVERANCE

SUPERSEDE

NOTICEABLE

Helpful hint: *Your sentence does not have to make sense. In fact, the sillier the better, as then it's more likely to stick in your mind.*

Task 2: Think of a mnemonic to help you remember the 12 disciples of Jesus Christ in chronological order: Bartholomew, Andrew, John, Philip, Thomas, Matthew, James the Great, James, Judas Iscariot, Simon Peter, Simon Zelotes, and Thaddaeus.

If this technique works for you, try to make up mnemonics to remember other useful facts and amaze your friends and family. You could also log on to a mnemonics Web site and learn some popular ones. Alternatively, post some of your own just for fun.

You can also use mnemonics to remember numbers. Simply choose words with the same number of letters as the number you are trying to remember. For example, to remember the telephone number 836–324–1424 think of: Crackers (8) and (3) cheese (6) for (3) me (2) with (4) a (1) drop (4) of (2) milk (4).

To really impress your friends, use the following mnemonic to remember *pi*—the complex number that expresses the ratio of the circumference of a circle to its diameter: 3.141592653 . . . May I have a large container of coffee? Thank you!

20 Seeing Things

Aim: To use a familiar place, such as your own home, as a visual memory aid.

Task 1: Imagine that you need to remember a list of things you have to do. Divide your list into sections: things to do at home, at the store, on the phone, and so on. Next, picture your home in your mind's eye and assign one room of your house to each section. Now, in your mind's eye, go to each room in your house and place a note about each task in different places in the room. When you need to remember your "to do" list again, in your mind's eye visit each room in your "house" and pick up the notes.

> *Helpful hint: If you make the image appropriate to the task, it will make your job easier. For example, if you want to remember to make a phone call, try leaving a note by the phone in your mind's eye. When you have retrieved your notes, dispose of them in an imaginary trash can so that you can use this technique again.*

Keep practicing this technique, as the more often you do it the better you'll get.

If remembering in pictures comes easily to you, try the following:

Task 2: Choose a road or street you know really well (such as the one you live on). Gather the information you need to remember, divide it into categories, and then in your mind's eye write each piece of information on a "For

Sale" sign. Now, again in your mind's eye, erect boards outside each house or store or familiar landmark on the street. Then, when you need to remember the information, take an imaginary walk down your street and read each sign and the information on it.

Now try using your body clock as a memory aid instead.

Task 3: Take a few days to study the natural rhythms of your life—the times you eat, sleep, work, rest, and play. When you are familiar with your routines, start to associate other activities with them. For instance, when you have your morning coffee break, use it as a signal to check your e-mails or make important phone calls and so on.

Human Encyclopedia

Aim: To stimulate your memory with fascinating facts.

It's easier to memorize things that interest you or that are unusual or stand out in some way.

Task: Review the list of unusual human facts below for five minutes. Then close the book and see how many you can recall.

- ❑ Women blink twice as many times as men do.
- ❑ We are about ⅓ inch taller in the morning than in the evening because the spongy discs that act as cushions between the vertebrae get compressed over the course of the day.
- ❑ There are approximately 550 hairs in one eyebrow.
- ❑ The strongest muscle (gram for gram) in the human body is the tongue.
- ❑ The world's youngest parents were aged eight and nine and lived in China in 1910.
- ❑ The largest kidney stone known weighed 3 pounds.
- ❑ Most dust particles in your house are fragments of dead skin.
- ❑ Babies are born without kneecaps. They appear when the child is two to six years of age.
- ❑ Your body creates and destroys 15 million red blood cells per second!
- ❑ The average human produces 10,000 gallons of saliva in a lifetime.

- If you ate too many carrots you would turn orange.
- The force created by one billion people jumping at the same time is equal to 500 tons of TNT.
- A baby is born every seven seconds.
- You breathe about 10 million times a year.
- The colder the room you sleep in, the better the chances are that you'll have a bad dream.
- The foot is the body part most commonly bitten by insects.
- The most common time for a wake-up call is 7 A.M.
- The nail on the middle finger grows faster than the nails on the other fingers.
- Your hearing is less sharp if you eat too much.
- You swallow around 300 times while eating dinner.
- More people are alive today than have ever died.
- The average male beard contains between 7,000 and 15,000 hairs.
- During an average lifetime, a man will spend 3,350 hours removing 27.5 feet of stubble.
- The hardest bone in the human body is the jawbone.

Helpful hint: You are more likely to remember something if it intrigues you. If you didn't find any of these facts particularly interesting, find other ways to broaden your mind, such as browsing an encyclopedia or surfing the Internet.

Curiosity is the key to all knowledge. If you managed to recall more than half of these unusual facts, you're ready to start taking more intellectual risks in your daily life. For example, if you have always wanted to start painting or write a novel, why not have a go now? Or sign up for an art or creative writing class. Read books you wouldn't normally read. Talk to people from different walks of life. Join a debating society or book club and make sure your voice is heard. Think of all this experimentation as an adventure.

If you could only recall up to five facts from this list, awaken your curiosity by learning something new. It doesn't matter what it is; the important point is that you begin to broaden your mind.

Measure your progress so far

❏ *Can you remember five details about your first day at a new school?*

❏ *Can you remember 10 details of your life when you first heard Princess Diana had died? For example, where were you living? Who were your friends? What did you enjoy doing in your free time?*

❏ *Without looking at your watch, write down what time it is.*

Just being able to answer one of these correctly is a sign that you are making great progress. Recalling something you haven't thought of for years or accurately predicting the time without needing a watch suggests that your memory is becoming much stronger and more adaptable.

There's a clear link between memory and confidence.

Think . . .

❏ *How much easier it is to start chatting with someone if you remember their name.*

❏ *How special it makes friends and loved ones feel when you remember their birthday or something important to them.*

❏ *How much easier it is to impress your boss or teacher if you can recall the details of interactions you've had with them in the past.*

❏ *How less stressful things are when you remember where you put your keys, your glasses, or your mobile phone.*

Life really is much richer and much easier when you can remember more of it.

Section 3
PROBLEM SOLVING

Studies have shown that logic and problem-solving exercises stimulate new neural pathways and patterns of mental activity that greatly enhance the way the brain functions. As your brain becomes more efficient at processing information, you become better able to deal with all sorts of mental tasks in daily life, not just puzzles. In order to achieve these brain-boosting benefits, you need to challenge your brain with problem-solving exercises on a regular basis.

If you find that you get easily confused in complex situations, that simple calculations, forms, and instructions are baffling, or that you just cannot spot the simple solutions to problems that others seem to grasp effortlessly, then this section is for you. It will help sharpen your logic and problem-solving skills.

Before you start, check your problem-solving abilities as they are at the moment. If you answer "yes" to more than 3 of the following 10 questions, you should pay special attention to this section.

❑ Did you struggle with math at school?
❑ Do you ever find yourself going around in circles trying to come up with a solution to a simple problem?

❑ Do you struggle when you have to work with figures?

❑ Do you find crossword puzzles difficult?

❑ Do questions involving logic make your head spin?

❑ Do you put off making decisions or prefer someone else to make them?

❑ Do you find IQ questions beyond you?

❑ Do you feel that your mental processes are slower than other people's?

❑ Do you feel you are always the last person to understand something or grasp the punchline of a joke?

❑ Is it hard for you to come up with creative solutions or new ideas?

22

Odd One Out

Aim: To boost the brain's ability to make logical connections.

Task 1: All the words (or letters) in the eight lines below appear at first glance to be closely related, but in fact there is an impostor in the list. Can you work out which one doesn't belong? You've got two minutes to figure it out!

Boston, Dallas, New York, Cinncinnati, Wyoming

April, Holly, Charity, Dandelion, Sandy, India

Tulip, Iris, Hyacinth, Crocus, Impatiens

A, F, I, E, O

Yard, Inch, Foot, Acre, Mile

Sundial, Watch, Clock, Barometer, Chronograph

Tennis, Volleyball, Ice Hockey, Football, Baseball

Thesaurus, Dictionary, Novel, Atlas, Encyclopedia

(Answers on page 223.)

> *Helpful hint: For each list, try to work out whether the connection is in the words/letters themselves or their order, or is there something else that connects them?*

If these lists didn't stump you and you got all the answers within the two minutes allowed, have a go at something a little different.

If you didn't manage to get more than two of these within the two minutes allowed, don't rush to look up the answers but instead return to them again a little later, several times if necessary. Each time you make your brain work that little bit harder you are creating new neural pathways that will make the next problem you tackle that much easier. If you continue to find this task hard after several attempts, try Exercise 23.

Task 2: The following letters relate to a series of words you are extremely familiar with. First, identify the words and then work out what the next letter in the list should be.

W, T, F, S, S, M, ?

(Answer on page 223.)

> **Helpful hint:** *Think of things that often come in sets, such as the months of the year, or the signs of the zodiac.*

Anagrams

Aim: To boost your word skills.

An anagram rearranges the letters of one word or phrase to make another word or phrase. For instance, an anagram for CLINT EASTWOOD could be OLD WEST ACTION.

Other examples:

TEACH = CHEAT

PALE = LEAP, PLEA, PEAL

ROMAN = A NORM, A MORN, NO ARM, MANOR

TEA CUP = APT CUE, CUT PEA

Task 1: You have five minutes to find out what the following five anagrams have in common:

MAY TAKE LACIE YACHT ARMY

(Answer on page 223.)

Helpful hint: Always use capital letters. Write the words backward or in a circle. This takes your mind off the original word and its meaning and helps you see the many options available. It may also help to write each letter on a small card and shuffle the cards around on the table.

If you solved this puzzle but it took you longer than five minutes, then strengthen your word skills with some extra practice, as follows.

Task 2: Whoever you meet today, try to come up with at least one anagram from his or her name.

If you solved the puzzle

within the five minutes allowed, there are numerous anagram Web sites to explore on the Internet. Alternatively, you can get a book of anagrams or verbal challenges from your local bookstore or library.

If this had you stumped then try this:

Task 3: Practice anagrams by writing your own first name down and see how many hidden words you can find. Then try using your first and last name. Now see how many words you can make out of the following: RETIREMENT, WASHINGTON, and CHRISTMAS.

Use Your Eyes

Aim: To strengthen your powers of visual reasoning.

Task 1: The diagram below shows a square with four coins on each side—rearrange the coins to make another square with five coins on each side (answer on page 224). You've got five minutes.

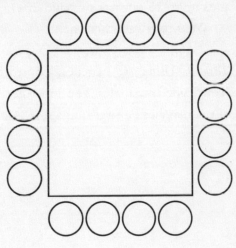

Helpful hint: Practice using real coins. If you still find this difficult, try to look at the problem in a different way. (There's no reason why coins can't be placed on top of one another!)

If you did this task within the five minutes allowed, your visual reasoning powers are in good shape. Did you use real coins in this exercise or work it out in your head? Here's another exercise to challenge you.

Task 2: The numbers one to nine below are positioned in a three-by-three square:

$$\begin{array}{ccc} 1 & 2 & 3 \\ 4 & 5 & 6 \\ 7 & 8 & 9 \end{array}$$

Rearrange them so that each row, column, and diagonal adds up to 15 (answer on page 224).

Want to try another one?

Task 3: Using six matches, construct four equilateral (equal-sided) triangles. You must not bend or break any of the matches (answer on page 224).

Number Magic

Aim: To refresh your left-brain skills.

Task 1: You've got 10 minutes to answer as many of the following questions as possible:

- ❏ Last year Simon was exactly six times as old as his son. This year he is exactly five times as old as his son. What will their ages be next year?
- ❏ Jane walks half a mile in 15 minutes. How far will she have gone in one and a half hours?
- ❏ Ten people at a meeting each shake hands with everyone present. How many handshakes will there be in total?
- ❏ Lisa is five feet six inches tall and weighed 170 pounds. She went on a diet for 10 weeks and lost three pounds each week. How much did she weigh at the end of the 10 weeks?
- ❏ The sum of the ages of three children in a family is 34. What will the sum of their ages be in three years time? (Answers on page 224.)

> *Helpful hint: There is no trick solution here; you just need persistence. If you have a natural feel for numbers, you should be able to answer these questions within the time given.*

Here's something else to challenge your left brain.

Task 2: The next time you go for a weekly shop at the supermarket, try to add up the prices of the items you are buying and see if you're correct when it's time to pay. If you find all this is a piece of cake, you might want to try your hand at Sudoku—the ultimate logic game (if you haven't gotten hooked already!).

If you struggled with some of these, it may help to limber up your left brain with some counting exercises.

Task 3: As fast as you can, count out loud in twos up to 100, then count down in twos from 100 to zero. Now try counting in threes up to 100 and back down again. For the ultimate challenge, count up and down in sevens.

Dodgy Logic

Aim: To enhance your reasoning powers by solving problems of logic.

Task 1: Answer the following logic questions. You've got four minutes.

- ❑ Letter is to envelope as foot is to: leg, hand, carry, sock, hat?
- ❑ Is it legal in South Dakota for a man to marry his widow's sister?
- ❑ In France, why can't you take a picture of a woman with hair curlers?
- ❑ Many hundreds of years ago a thief was charged with treason against a Roman emperor and sentenced to death. The emperor, feeling merciful, asked the man how he would like to die. Which way would you choose to die if you found yourself in the same situation?
- ❑ Elizabeth has six pairs of black gloves and six pairs of brown gloves in her drawer. In complete darkness how many gloves must she take out to make sure she has a matching pair? (Answers on page 224.)

Helpful hint: There's no catch here. All the information you need to answer these questions correctly can be found in the question. No specialized knowledge or mathematical skill is required, just the ability to think clearly and analytically.

If this really clicked with you, you're the kind of person who can see through details and get to what is essential. Here's a very tricky challenge that will stretch your left brain to the max.

Task 2: A man lives on the tenth floor of a building. Every day he takes the elevator down to the ground floor to go to work or to go shopping. When he returns, if he is alone in the elevator he takes it to the seventh floor and walks up the stairs to reach his apartment on the tenth floor. When he is with someone, he rides in the elevator all the way to the tenth floor. When it's raining outside, he also rides to the tenth, whether he is alone in the elevator or not. He hates climbing stairs, so why does he do it? (Answer on page 225.)

Chess is a fantastic way to boost your logic skills and reasoning power as well as your concentration and problem-solving skills. It also happens to be an exciting and addictive hobby! If you don't already know how to play the game, why not learn and teach friends or family so you can all play together?

27 Never Assume!

Aim: To be more flexible in your thinking.

Task 1: Solve the following. In each of these puzzles you are given some clues to a scenario, but the clues don't tell the full story. Your job is to fill in the details and complete the stories below. You've got 10 minutes, tops!

❑ A man and his son are driving home from a football game when they have a terrible accident. The man is taken to the intensive care department and the boy is taken straight to the operating room. The surgeon comes over to the operating table, sees the boy and says, "I can't operate on this patient, he's my son!" How can this be?

❑ A woman throws something out of a window and dies. How did this happen?

❑ What is both the longest and the shortest thing in the world, the fastest and the slowest, the most neglected and the most regretted, without which nothing can be done?

> *Helpful hint: To complete the stories you need to be flexible in your thinking, step outside your normal mode of thought, and attack the problem from a different direction. Bear in mind, too, that sometimes a problem seems difficult or insoluble because our assumptions are wrong. To solve these puzzles you'll need to challenge your assumptions, especially about who? what? when? where? and why?*

❏ A man married five women, but stayed single all his life. How? (Answers on page 225.)

If this was all transparently obvious to you, well done! The next insurance salesman or used-car dealer who tries to pull the wool over your eyes won't stand a chance. Now, try the following lateral-thinking game with a friend.

Task 2: Choose two objects at random and combine them in a novel way. See who can come up with the best idea. What can you come up with, for example, from the combination of a car and a microwave? Perhaps a car that has a built-in microwave or microwaveable-ready meals in the shape of a car?

If you found the logic problems in Task 1 too difficult, you may be making too many assumptions. Try to keep an open mind and be more flexible in your thinking. You'll also benefit from the Creativity exercises in Section Five (see page 94).

28

Calculation

Aim: To strengthen your problem-solving skills.

Task 1: Use all the digits from one to nine and any combination of plus and minus signs to add up to 100. The digits must be used in the correct order: 1, 2, 3, 4, 5, 6, 7, 8, 9 (answer on page 225). You've got five minutes.

Helpful hint:
There's no shortcut here. You need to concentrate and work logically until you get the answer.

If you worked this out easily, here's something to test both your thinking and numerical skills. It might just get you chewing your pencil.

Task 2: Two mothers and two daughters went for lunch. They bought a giant pizza and divided it into equal parts using three straight cuts. They then had equal shares of the pizza. How did they do this? (Answer on page 225.)

If you found these harder than you expected, have a go at Exercise 31. Or perhaps you need to put in more practice with the Concentration exercises in Section One (see page 4), as the secret to this kind of exercise is persistence. Here's another challenge:

Task 3: Try reciting the two-times table out loud while writing down the three-times table.

Eureka!

Aim: To enhance lateral reasoning skills by means of logic problems.

Task 1: Connect these nine points together using four straight lines, but without lifting your pen or pencil from the paper.

O   O   O

O   O   O

O   O   O

(Answer on page 225.)

> *Helpful hint: For this task you need to think outside the box—quite literally!*

If you find you need more than five minutes for this, it might help to take a break and come back to the question later. You might also review Exercise 27: Never Assume!

If you managed this okay, you'll probably enjoy the next two as well.

Task 2: What do the following words all have in common?

Buy   Catch   Bring   Seek   Teach   Think

(Answer on page 225.)

> *Helpful hint: Think of sounds rather than meanings here.*

Task 3: Solve this conundrum. You buy it, though you don't really want one. If you can't afford to buy it, you are given one. It protects you even though you don't need protection. It keeps working long after it has been disposed of. What is it? (Answer on page 226.)

30 Birthday Party

Aim: To solve problems using a combination of logic, persistence, and concentration.

Task: From the clues below, work out whose child is whose and their relevant ages. At a recent birthday party there were four mothers and their children, aged 1, 2, 3, and 4. It was Jane's child's birthday party. Brian is not the oldest child. Sarah had Anne just over a year ago. Laura's child will be 3 next birthday. Daniel is older than Charlie. Teresa's child is the oldest. Charlie is older than Laura's child (answer on page 226).

If you managed this one, don't get complacent—keep practicing. Give your "mental muscles" another boost with the next exercise—Picturing.

If you found this difficult, you may be making things more complicated than they need to be. In most problems like this there is a simple answer or formula; it's just a matter of finding it. Bear in mind that success in solving logic problems often depends not so much on brain power but on persistence. You may also benefit from reviewing the Concentration exercises in Section One (see page 4).

Helpful hint: To solve this, draw a couple of tables: one for the ages and the children's names and the other for the children's names and mothers' names. For example:

Age?

	Brian
Child's name	*Anne*
	Daniel
	Charlie

Mother's name?

	Brian
Child's name	*Anne*
	Daniel
	Charlie

31 Picturing

Aim: To tackle logic problems using pictorial skills.

Task: A modern artist has 10 identical statues that are to be exhibited in one room of a gallery. The artist insists that there are three statues against each of the four walls.

How would you arrange the figures? You've got two minutes (answer on page 226).

Helpful hint: You can solve this problem easily by drawing several rectangles and experimenting using dots to indicate the statues.

If you managed this task, you could give your brain a treat by visiting an art museum, or even creating a piece of art yourself. Paying attention to artistic details is a great way to boost your thinking skills.

While some people cope best with tasks that require visual skills, others may prefer hearing or physical skills. If you found this task difficult, you may not be sight-oriented so much as hearing- or doing-oriented. Once you know which type you are, you can work out the best way to learn, remember, concentrate, and apply yourself. If writing things down does not help you to learn new facts, you might find it easier to process information if you *listen* to it. Try saying it out loud or recording it onto a tape recorder and playing it back to yourself several times. You could also try talking to yourself while reading or learning something new or trying to solve a puzzle. Exercising your brain by listening to lots of great music can help, too.

If you are a doing-oriented type, you will do best by acting out, experiencing, or doing whatever it is you are trying to learn. You might find it easier to solve exercises such as the statue task above if you "get physical." For example, you might ask 10 friends to stand in a room so that you can move them about. If that isn't practical, you could move marbles or coins about on a piece of paper.

Measure your progress so far

Think of a question that you don't know the answer to. For example:

☐ *Why is the sky blue?*
☐ *Why do stars twinkle?*
☐ *Why do men have nipples?*
☐ *What would life be like if time ran backward?*

Now ask three people for their opinions. When you have all three answers, settle on the one that you believe to be correct. If you are still not satisfied, seek out more advice.

Whether or not the answer you eventually decide on is correct or incorrect doesn't really matter. What is important here is your approach. If you thought about the question yourself, and then sought out the opinions of at least three other people to see if you had missed anything obvious, this is a clear sign that your problem-solving skills have taken a big leap forward.

Section 4
COMMUNICATION

effective communication is essential for success in all areas of life, so if you often find it difficult to express yourself clearly and logically or feel that people sometimes misunderstand you, then this is the section for you.

The exercises in this section are designed to stimulate neurotransmitters and neural connections in the left side of the brain, where verbal ability and communication skills are mainly concentrated. If you need some extra help, you'll find hints and tips after the exercises that should spur you on. Some of the exercises must be performed with the help of a friend or group of friends. Sometimes the messages you send are nonverbal. There are communication tasks here to improve both verbal and nonverbal communication skills.

Before you start, check your powers of communication as they are at the moment. If you answer "yes" to more than 3 of the following 10 questions, you should pay special attention to this section.

❑ Do you often find it a struggle to choose the right words?

❑ Do people often look confused when you speak to them?

❏ Do you feel uncomfortable in social situations?

❏ Do you sometimes take ages to get to the point?

❏ Do you find it difficult to put across your point of view?

❏ Do you often feel as if the word you want is on the tip of your tongue?

❏ Do you find it hard to express yourself?

❏ Do you loathe speaking in public?

❏ Do you get nervous if you have to ask a stranger for directions?

❏ Do you get flustered if you make a call and get an answering machine/voice mail?

32

Charades

Aim: To enhance nonverbal communication skills.

Task: Play charades with family or friends. Here are the basic rules. You're probably familiar with them already, but they are outlined again below as a helpful reminder.

The audience will ask you what the subject is. To reply you use one of the following gestures—whichever one applies:

❑ Book title: Put your hands together and then open them like a book.
❑ Movie title: Pretend to crank an old-fashioned movie camera.
❑ Play title: Mime a theater curtain opening.
❑ Song title: Pretend to sing.
❑ TV show: Draw a rectangle to outline the TV screen.
❑ Quote or phrase: Make quotation marks in the air with your fingers.

You must now describe your subject to the audience without speaking, just using mime. Use the following hand gestures to indicate:

❑ The number of words in the title: Hold up that number of fingers.
❑ Which word you're miming: Hold up the number of fingers that indicate first, second, third word, and so on.
❑ The number of syllables in a word: As above, but lay that number of fingers on your arm.

❑ Which syllable you're miming: Lay that number of fingers on your arm again.

❑ A small word: Hold up finger and thumb.

❑ A big word: Hold your hands apart, as though describing a big fish you've caught.

❑ The: Place one hand on top of the upright fingers of the other in a "T" sign.

❑ The whole title or phrase: Draw a circle with your hands.

❑ A word that sounds like the actual word: Cup one hand behind your ear.

❑ A longer version of: Pretend to stretch a piece of elastic.

❑ A shorter version of: Do a karate chop with your hand.

❑ Plural: Link your little fingers.

❑ Past tense: Wave your hand over your shoulder toward your back.

❑ A letter of the alphabet: Move your hand in a chopping motion toward your arm (near the top of your forearm if the letter is near the beginning of the alphabet, and near the bottom of your arm if the letter is near the end of the alphabet).

❑ That a guess is nearly right: Wave your hands.

❑ A correctly guessed word: Tap your nose.

❑ A completely correct answer: Put one finger on your nose while pointing at the winner with your other hand.

Remember, for the purpose of mental fitness this is all about *non*verbal communication. You've got five minutes to mime your chosen subject to your audience and for them to guess what it is. If at any time during the game you say, or even grunt, anything, the other team or person wins. So lips sealed!

33 Forbidden Words

Aim: To improve your mastery with words.

Task: Try to describe the four words below without using certain forbidden words—or your hands. For example, if "rectangle" was the chosen word, you wouldn't be able to use the words "four," "square," "oblong," and "right angle" to describe it, or mime a square with your hands. This task works best if you describe the word to a friend or family member. See if they can guess each word within one minute.

☐ Sphere: Forbidden words—ball, round, globe, circle.
☐ Parallel: Forbidden words—direction, line, equals, straight.
☐ Circle: Forbidden words—round, 360, radius, ball.
☐ Triangle: Forbidden words—pyramid, three, equilateral, point.

If you enjoyed doing this, choose some more words or phrases and list the words most commonly used to describe them. Have fun using unfamiliar ways to describe something familiar.

Gone in Sixty Seconds

Aim: To enhance your ability to communicate clearly and concisely.

Task: Choose a subject and talk about it for 60 seconds. It can be anything from the weather to your favorite novel. Set a timer so that you know when the minute is up. If you hesitate, stop talking, say "um" or "ah," repeat what you have said, or digress from the subject, then you haven't succeeded and need to reset the timer and start again. It's best to play this with other people so they can judge your performance and interrupt if you make a mistake. If you are playing it alone, use a tape recorder to record what you are saying. Then you can play it back and analyze your own performance. A version of this is played on the long-running BBC Radio 4 game show, *Just a Minute*, except that someone else sets the subject and whoever interrupts has to take over. Why not get friends or family together and give it a try?

35 Word Power

Aim: To build your vocabulary.

Task: Think of words that fit the criteria given below. This is a great game to play with children and it will benefit their word skills, too. If you find these easy, shorten the time limit to challenge yourself to think more quickly. Have a go at one, or all, of the following.

❑ List all the things you can think of that are invisible. Love, germs, air, anger are just a few. Try to think of at least 20 invisible things, then build up to 30, 50, or even 100!

❑ Recite the alphabet out loud, attaching a word to each letter. For example A—animal, B—boat, C—cat, and so on. Now go through the alphabet again, this time attaching two words to each letter. Repeat, but this time try to do it as fast as you can. When you are ready, attach three, then four, then five words to each letter.

❑ Using a kitchen timer, see how many five-letter words you can write down in two minutes. Now try six-letter words.

❑ Write the letters of the alphabet, A to Z, down the left-hand margin of a sheet of paper. Put a different letter on each line. Beside each letter, write a word beginning with that letter that is related to holidays. If you prefer to use another theme, just substitute something else. The theme doesn't matter. The idea is to challenge your brain. You may find it tough when you get to q, x, and z, but keep trying.

36

Trust Walk

Aim: To test your ability to communicate clearly and effectively.

Task: Get a friend to work on this exercise with you. One of you should be blindfolded and the other sighted. The sighted person cannot touch the blindfolded person and is completely responsible for the care and safety of their partner. Designate the time for each person to be blindfolded before switching, say two to three minutes. Both people should walk slowly together using only verbal communication to move forward and change direction. The sighted person is responsible for all verbal directional commands.

As the sighted person in this exercise you will need to master the art of verbal communication and guide your partner without prodding or poking them! Good verbal skill is the key factor when guiding your partner, but you also need authority and clarity to inspire confidence in your partner, who will probably feel very vulnerable and insecure in a trust walk.

As the blindfolded person in this exercise you will be disoriented and will have to listen carefully and follow your partner's instructions word for word. Because you cannot see, you will have to make full use of all your other senses, such as hearing and touch.

37 Body Talk

Aim: To further enhance nonverbal communication skills.

Task: Ask a colleague, partner, or family member to help you with this exercise. You have two minutes to communicate the following using nonverbal communications only. You can only move on to b) when the person working with you has guessed a) correctly and so on until you reach j).

a) No
b) Sit down
c) Come in
d) Be quiet
e) I don't know
f) Go away or get away
g) Stand up
h) I'm mad
i) I'm happy
j) Stop

Story Time

Aim: To improve communication skills and creativity.

Task 1: Grab a few friends or family members and play the Story Time game. One player begins by saying, "We went on vacation last week." The next player must continue the story, beginning with "unfortunately," such as, "Unfortunately, we forgot our passports." The next player continues with a statement beginning with "fortunately," such as, "Fortunately, one of us remembered in time." Continue around the group, alternating between "unfortunately" and "fortunately."

Task 2: Write a short paragraph that incorporates the following unrelated words:

Woman, television, plant, igloo, lightbulb, snake, massage, rocket, mouse, van, book, plate, glue, finger, spoon

Other words can be used to complete the sentences. To continue the challenge, choose 15 more unrelated words and repeat the exercise.

39

Tongue Twisters

Aim: To use alliteration to enhance linguistic skills.

Task: Say the familiar Peter Piper tongue twister, beginning slowly and gradually and building up speed until you can say the words as fast as you can.

> *Peter Piper picked a peck of pickled peppers.*
> *Did Peter Piper pick a peck of pickled peppers?*
> *If Peter Piper picked a peck of pickled peppers,*
> *Where's the peck of pickled peppers Peter Piper picked?*

Now try some more:

> *She sells seashells by the seashore.*
> *The shells she sells are surely seashells.*
> *So if she sells shells on the seashore,*
> *I'm sure she sells seashore shells.*

> *Which wristwatches are Swiss wristwatches?*

> *How much wood would a woodchuck chuck*
> *If a woodchuck could chuck wood?*
> *He would chuck, he would, as much as he could,*
> *And chuck as much as a woodchuck would*
> *If a woodchuck could chuck wood.*

> *I slit the sheet, the sheet I slit: Now open the slitted sheet*
> *I slit.* (Be very careful with this one!)

If you're enjoying all these, why not try composing some tongue twisters of your own?

40

Have You Heard the One ...

Aim: To stimulate your verbal skills using humorous wordplay.

Task: Have a go at writing some jokes, even if you don't think you have a talent for comedy. One way to do this is to choose a form of behavior and take it to the extreme or exaggerate the effect. For example, you could compare your partner's snoring to an earthquake. This isn't a hilarious example, but you get the idea. You could also start with a word or a subject, and then fit it into various joke and riddle types such as opposite meanings of the same word, similarities between that word and something else, and so on. Here are some funny sayings to get you in joke-writing mood:

❑ Everybody lies. But it doesn't matter, since nobody listens.
❑ He who laughs last thinks slowest.
❑ Everyone has a photographic memory. Some just don't have any film.
❑ A day without sunshine is like, well, night.
❑ On the other hand you have different fingers.
❑ Change is inevitable—except from a vending machine.
❑ Honk if you love peace and quiet.
❑ Despite the cost of living, have you noticed how it remains so popular?
❑ It is hard to understand how a cemetery raised its burial costs and blamed it on the cost of living.

❑ A fine is a tax for doing wrong. A tax is a fine for doing well.

❑ I started out with nothing, and I still have most of it.

❑ Light travels faster than sound. This is why some people appear bright until you hear them speak.

❑ Before you criticize someone, you should walk a mile in their shoes. That way, when you criticize them, you are a mile away and you have their shoes.

❑ Why is it when we talk to God we're praying, but when God talks to us we're schizophrenic?

❑ Sticks and stones may break my bones but words . . . might hurt me deeply, causing great emotional, mental, and psychological damage leading to lowered self-esteem and decreased work-related efficiency.

❑ Always remember you're unique. Just like everyone else.

❑ It may be that your sole purpose in life is simply to serve as a bad example.

❑ They laughed when I said I wanted to be a comedian. They're not laughing now!

You may think you can't write jokes and riddles, but that might be because you have never tried. This is your chance. Go on—do it for a laugh.

Cracking the Code

Aim: To break down obstacles to communication.

Task 1: Can you decode the following cryptograms? They all follow the same rule:

Ni lkna rfnim ajnebse xat dn ahta ed tp ecxenia, treceb otdia seb nacgn.—Ihtondlr Owsihtni

Nilkn arf nima j nebdae, de ram eh tfoo wtf iter. —Cesapeek Yameerht

No tg nihsaw eg roege no dabana htes u cxe onr. —Effoot Rettebsiti

(Answers on page 226.)

If you got this right away you'll certainly enjoy logging on to some cryptogram Web sites. If it all looks Greek to you, practice your code-breaking skills with the following:

Task 2: Ask someone to write five short sentences and scramble the words. For example, "We all went to the park to take the dog for a walk," becomes "to the dog we all for a park went to the walk take." Now have a go at deciphering each sentence. When you've done that a few times you'll find it gets easier and easier to unlock the hidden message.

If you found most of the exercises in this section came naturally to you, you have a way with words. Keep nurturing and challenging your special gift. It's an excellent tool that will take you to magical places. If, on the other hand, you found it tough going, the following tips should help boost your verbal skills.

❑ Read as widely as possible. This is an excellent way to improve your vocabulary and will do wonders for your imagination as well! Choose a newspaper or magazine as different from the usual as possible, or read a book genre you have never tried before.

❑ Crossword puzzles, word searches, anagrams, quizzes, riddles, and Scrabble can all help to increase your vocabulary and enhance your literacy skills. Aim to do one or more puzzles a day, and vary the ones you try.

❑ Every day, challenge your mind to make a long list and keep adding to that list all day. For example, list as many birds, trees, or flowers as you can.

❑ Make a list of five important events in history and write a short paragraph about each event, explaining why it should be considered the most important. You can do the same with famous people, books, sporting events, poems, and so on.

❑ Get together with friends or family and play a game of Call My Bluff. Take turns to choose an obscure word from the dictionary and come up with three possible meanings. Two meanings should be bogus. Your challenge is to guess the correct one.

❑ Learn a new word a day and make sure you use it at least twice in conversation that day.

❑ Read an article in a newspaper and paraphrase (summarize) it in five short sentences.

Finally, the best way to enhance verbal intelligence and develop word skills is with practice. Find different ways to communicate. Pick up the phone instead of sending an e-mail, speak to the store salesperson, join in conversations at work (but don't butt in!). Interact with friends, family, colleagues, and the world around you. Make sure your voice is heard.

Measure your progress so far

Think about something you have done or said or some habit or quirk you have that is funny. If you can't think of anything right away, dig deep and search for the humor. It is there. Think like a comedian and poke fun at yourself. Don't put yourself down too much—just have a gentle laugh at your own expense.

If you managed to do this, congratulations! Your communications skills have improved greatly. Laughter releases stress and tension and makes it so much easier for you to relate to others and for others to relate to you.

Section 5
CREATIVITY

We are all born with a creative spark, but rarely are we taught how to nurture it. The exercises in this section will enhance and develop your creative ability. They are designed to stimulate the neurotransmitters and create new neural connections in the right side of your brain, the area associated with creativity and intuition. If you feel you need encouragement or want helpful tips, you'll find some creative solutions after the exercises.

Before you start, check your level of creative ability at the moment. If you answer "yes" to more than 3 of the following 10 questions, you should pay special attention to this section.

❑ Do you find it hard to come up with new ideas?
❑ Are you a creature of habit?
❑ Have you worn the same clothes or had the same hair style for the last five years?
❑ Would you describe yourself as conventional?
❑ Do you sometimes wish you could be more spontaneous?
❑ At school, did you hate creative writing exercises or arts subjects in general?
❑ Does change make you feel uncomfortable?
❑ Do you feel as if you are stuck in a rut?
❑ Does your work give you little scope to express yourself?
❑ Do you travel to the same vacation destination every year?

42

What If?

Aim: To boost your imaginative skills.

The key to using your imagination to the full is to act as if the imagined scene were real and already happening. Instead of pretending, imagine it as though you are truly experiencing it in the present—as a real event in the here and now.

Task 1: Think of anything about your life that you would like to change or enhance. Sit back, relax, close your eyes, and imagine how you would really like your life to be in that regard. Don't put any limitations on it, and don't shroud it with doubt. Remember, no one else is going to judge this fantasy and no one else is going to prevent it from happening. Only you have the power to stop it. Make it real in your mind.

Most of the time we try to think rational, realistic thoughts, but for the following task, give yourself permission to think crazy thoughts. Be as freewheeling and as far-fetched as you like.

Task 2: Write down three answers to each of the following questions:

❑ What if animals could talk?
❑ What if we never had to sleep?
❑ What if everyone lived to be 500?
❑ What if I were a genius?
❑ What if I could read other people's minds?
❑ What if I were president?

You may have thought of your own "What ifs" by now.

43

Brainstorming

Aim: To unlock your creative potential.

Task: Pick one or more of the following and come up with as many ideas as you can to solve the problem. When you think you have exhausted all possibilities, dig deeper and try to come up with a few more ideas. Aim to find at least 20 solutions for each problem. Bear in mind that no idea is too ridiculous when you brainstorm. Enjoy stimulating your brain to be creative.

What would you do if . . .

❑ Your boss started making impossible demands on your time?

❑ You were on a flight to England and the passenger next to you kept talking to you when all you wanted to do was read a book?

❑ You were asked for new ways to improve on the design of women's tights?

❑ You wanted to buy something but couldn't afford it?

❑ You needed to stop worrying?

❑ You wanted to make a positive difference in the world?

❑ Someone you like was ignoring you and you wanted to get them to notice you?

Now think of another problem, big or small, and brainstorm it.

44

Putty in Your Hands

Aim: To enhance creativity using a physical medium.

Task: Get your hands on some Play-Doh or modeling clay and try to make something that a friend or family member can recognize. This isn't about artistic skill but creative ability. Let's say you want to make a rabbit. There are many ways to suggest this that don't involve molding a perfect-looking rabbit. For example, making long ears and placing them on your head, or making buck teeth and putting them in your mouth.

If modeling isn't your thing, here's another simple creative exercise anyone can do. Gather together some household odds and ends, such as nuts, bolts, cartons, yogurt containers, and so on. Then use them to make a sculpture. It doesn't have to look like anything in partic-ular and can be purely abstract. Just try to make it look aesthetically pleasing. If you are stuck for ideas, just ask any three- or four-year-old to give you a few tips!

45

50 Words

Aim: To enhance creativity and concise communication.

Task: Write a complete story—with a beginning, a middle, and an end—in 50 words! This isn't impossible! Give it a try. One way to do this would be to compose a longer story and then find ways to cut it down until you end up with something pithy and entertaining. Most people need several attempts at this, so don't give up if it doesn't work the first time around.

Alternatively, you could get four or five friends or family members to sit in a circle with the aim of working in cooperation to produce an interesting story. Decide how long each person's turn is going to last and who is going to start. You may also want to decide on the theme of your story and whether you are going for realism or fantasy.

46 Cloud Watching

Aim: To expand your mind.

Intuition and flashes of insight tend to emerge when you let your mind wander and give your imagination freedom to experiment.

Task: Go outside and let your imagination run free as you explore the shapes that clouds make in the sky. Don't stare too intently at the clouds; just look at them vaguely—as though you were daydreaming. Just stay relaxed and see what shapes appear. If you look long enough, you will see images emerge. People often see faces, but you may notice other things. See how many different images you can identify and make a list of them all. Be sure to walk around and look at the whole sky because you'll see different images from various angles. When a particular cloud formation catches your eye, ask yourself: "What does that image look like to me? What does it mean to me?"

Warning: Take great care to avoid looking directly at the sun. On a sunny day, wear good quality sunglasses and look in a part of the sky well away from the sun.

47 Doodlebug

Aim: To use doodling to unlock your creative subconscious.

Task: Take a piece of paper and doodle on it. Just let yourself go. You don't have to have a particular image in mind. The idea is to let your pencil roam freely over the page and just see what happens. Focus your mind on it and see where your imagination takes you. After a few minutes, take a look at what you've done. You may be surprised at how creative you've been. If drawing just isn't your thing, a variation on this theme is to cut pictures from magazines and make a collage. This may seem like something a child would do (you probably did it yourself when you were little) but can be very satisfying. The aim is not to produce a prize-winning piece of art but simply to get in touch with your neglected creative side.

48 Go Dotty!

Aim: To be more creative by forcing yourself to be uncreative!

This task is fascinating and can be traced back to the paintings of ancient China. It aims to encourage creativity by forcing you to be as deliberately uncreative and unimaginative as possible. Sound interesting? Why not give it a try?

Task 1: Take a sheet of paper, black ink, and a brush. Your task is to put dots and splashes of ink on the paper in a random way, without making a pattern. Sounds easy, doesn't it? Yet the harder you try not to make a pattern, the more a pattern will begin to emerge. Your creative powers just won't allow you to stifle them.

When you've finished, here's another exercise.

Task 2: Fold a sheet of paper down the center. Put a drop of ink in the fold and then press the two sides together. Unfold it and see what shape you have formed. What do you see in the design?

While on the subject of dots, have a go at the following dot creativity task.

Task 3: On a clean sheet of paper, make a large black dot and ask yourself, "What is it?" Let your imagination go wild. A child might see a distant star, a squashed insect, and so on. Try to think like a child again.

49

Change Contexts

Aim: To dig deep to find a hidden well of creativity.

Task: Think of 30 possible uses for a paper clip. For example, in an office, a paper clip is normally used to hold paper together—but a thief might use it to pick a lock, or an engineer might use it to connect cables, and so on. By changing the context in which the paper clip is used, you investigate possibilities beyond the obvious and explore your creativity. The reason you need to come up with 30 possible uses is that after the first 5 or 6 ideas you'll find you have to dig much deeper to come up with more. You can repeat this exercise with any household item: the cardboard tube in a toilet paper roll, a spool, an empty plastic bottle, a lightbulb, and so on.

50

Someone Else's Shoes

Aim: To find new ways to overcome creative blocks.

Task: Instead of thinking about a problem from your own perspective, try to look at it from a different and unfamiliar point of view. In other words, think of the problem as though you were in someone else's shoes. You can choose anyone you like: someone you know, someone currently famous, such as a television celebrity, or even a historical figure, such as Napoleon or Queen Elizabeth I. By seeing the familiar from an unfamiliar perspective, you encourage the brain to make original connections, and this can often trigger ideas that would not otherwise have occurred to you. If you find this technique helps you come up with creative solutions, explore other famous personalities and see what new ideas emerge from their perspective.

51

On the Edge

Aim: To tap in to your semiconscious state and allow your creativity to surface.

In that twilight world when you are about to fall asleep, flashes of inspiration are more likely to surface. The problem is that most of us do then fall asleep and so forget what images we may have glimpsed. The surrealist artist Salvador Dalí found a way to overcome this. He would doze off in an armchair with a metal spoon in his hand held directly over a metal dish he had placed on the floor. As soon as he fell asleep he dropped the spoon and the clatter as it hit the dish would wake him up. He was then able to remember vividly what he had just experienced in his semiconscious state.

Task: Have a go yourself. Make sure that when you wake up you write down your ideas right away or the inspiration will vanish from your memory.

To boost your creativity, the best thing you can do is to believe you are creative. This will send your mind in the right direction. From now on, never question that you have a creative gift and use everything you say, think, dream, write, draw, do, feel, hear, taste, and smell to enhance your creativity. Hold on to all your ideas. Here are a few more things you can do to awaken your creativity:

❑ Keep a notebook or pen and paper handy and regularly write down your thoughts and ideas.

❏ Study your dreams; they can be a good source of inspiration.

❏ Have plenty of new experiences to feed your mind and your creativity.

❏ Listen to what is going on around you or to what other people say, as this can all trigger bright ideas.

❏ Laugh more. This is an excellent frame of mind to encourage creative thought. Don't take yourself too seriously either; ego stifles creativity. Humor embellishes the unusual, and this is where creativity springs from.

❏ Pay attention to feelings of envy, as it is often a message from your creative core. What talent would you like to have? What has triggered your envy? How could you develop your creativity in that area?

❏ Quiet time: To reach your inner wellspring of creativity you need to be able to set aside your ego temporarily to allow your intuition and inspiration to take center stage. So set aside some quiet time every day to reflect and let your mind drift and your imagination soar. Meditation is one way to do this. The exercises in Section One: Concentration will help.

Measure your progress so far

At some point this week, read a science fiction or fantasy story. If you haven't got much free time this week, watch an episode of Doctor Who. *Allow yourself to become immersed in the worlds that science fiction and fantasy writers have created. If you manage to do this, you are allowing yourself to contemplate the impossible and dwell in parallel universes and so have found a great way to unlock your creativity. In Lewis Carroll's* Alice in Wonderland, *The Queen of Hearts advised Alice to believe one impossible thing every day before breakfast. That's good advice.*

Section 6
REACTION TIME

ever get the feeling it's now taking you that split second longer to react when you're driving, playing sports, or catching a falling vase? Or you're no longer so quick with a witty comeback? Well, there's so much you can do to stay quick, sharp, and witty for longer.

The exercises in this section are all designed to improve hand–eye coordination, which in turn encourages the development of new neural pathways and connections and improves your reaction time and your ability to think fast under pressure. Your mission is to have a go at all of them and then, a day later, to come back and do them again to see if you can improve on your time and/or your performance. Keep going until you are speed thinking and reacting like a Formula One racing driver. If you need a boost, you'll find some helpful tips at the end of the section.

Before you start, check your reactions as they are at the moment. If you answer "yes" to more than 3 of the following 10 questions, you should pay special attention to this section.

❑ Do you feel that the world is getting faster?
❑ Do you get beeped at more when you're driving?

❑ Do you find it hard to concentrate on one thing?

❑ Do you find yourself forgetting important numbers, such as your PIN number?

❑ Do you regularly get lost because your sense of direction is poor?

❑ Do you often drop things?

❑ Do you think you are accident prone?

❑ Have you been getting more points on your driver's license recently?

❑ Are you hopeless at computer and PlayStation games?

❑ Do friends often call you absentminded?

Catch It!

Aim: To test and improve your reaction times.

Task: Take a large piece of thick cardboard, some scissors, a ruler, and a pen or pencil. Cut the cardboard so that it is at least 8 inches long and 2 inches wide and mark as illustrated.

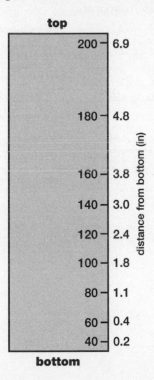

Write the numbers 40 to 200 (the time in milliseconds) on the card as shown, numbering up from the bottom of the card. This is your "reaction timer." Ask a friend to hold the reaction timer at the top. Line up your fingers with the bottom edge. Now ask your friend to drop the reaction timer, without warning, and you must try to grab it between your fingers. Don't chase it; that's cheating! Now read off your score from the side. The number indicates your reaction time in milliseconds.

Speed (milliseconds)	Rating
40	Excellent!
60	Very good
80	Good
100	Average
120	Below average
140	Slow
160	Very slow
180	Keep practicing—you'll get there!

53

Speedy Reading

Aim: To sharpen your scanning and observation skills.

Task: Choose any paragraph in a newspaper, set your timer to one minute, and use a pencil to cross out as quickly as you can all the *t*'s you can find in that text. Now choose another paragraph and cross out all the *c*'s. Now go back and review what you have done. You'll probably find that you missed some of the targeted letters. Try again the next day and keep practicing this exercise with different paragraphs and letters of the alphabet until you can strike out all the letters you are looking for.

54

Have a Ball

Aim: To use fun ways to improve your reaction time.

Task 1: Cut out a variety of letters, small shapes, and colored pieces of paper, and tape them to a ball or bean-bag. Then play catch with a friend, or bounce the ball off a wall, if you are on your own, spotting and calling out one or more of the colors, shapes, or objects before you catch the ball.

Task 2: Find a chalkboard or piece of paper, draw a large square, and divide it up into 16 smaller squares. Write the numbers 1 to 16 at random in the squares. Turn on your favorite music and point to each of the numbers in numerical order, keeping time with the beat. Try it again, this time working backward.

Task 3: Play snap. Snap is a fun and simple card game that can help you boost your reaction time. The game is played by two players. Each player takes a turn to lay down a card face up. If any card is the same value as the one played previously, the first person to spot it calls "snap" and places a hand on top of the pile. He or she then takes all the cards that have been played so far. The aim is to make your opponent run out of cards. The key is to react as quickly as possible.

55

Eye Exercises

Aim: To improve visual skills and reaction time and strengthen hand–eye coordination.

Task 1: Stand or sit in a relaxed posture. Hold a pencil at arm's length directly in front of your nose. Focus both eyes on the pencil and slowly move it toward you. Try to keep your eyes fixed on it all the way to your nose. Now move the pencil away from your face until it is at arm's length again. If your eyes drift away from the pencil, begin the exercise again. For optimal effectiveness, repeat this exercise 10 times, but stop if your eyes get tired.

Task 2: Stand or sit in a relaxed posture. Hold a pencil one foot in front of your face. Focus both eyes on the pencil and move it in an arc to the right side of your head until it is level with your ear. As you do this, keep your eyes fixed on the pencil until it is out of your field of vision— but without moving your head. Now bring the pencil back to the starting position, trying to keep it in focus all the way. Now repeat

Note: Neither of these tasks will actually improve your vision. They are short, simple movements that can help relieve eye strain or fatigue, improve hand–eye coordination, and contribute to the overall health of your eyes. In this way they can help make you more productive while reading or working at the computer—the two main causes of eye strain.

the task, this time on the left side. Repeat this task five times on each side. It is not uncommon for the pencil tip to become blurry or appear double as it approaches your nose, but try to do your best to keep it in sharp focus all the time.

56

Zap Some Aliens

Aim: To improve your mental and motor skills.

Task: Have a go at a PlayStation or computer game. If you've never played one before, you may feel a bit over-whelmed at first, but with practice you'll soon be a whiz. Don't get hooked on computer games and PlayStation, though, as too much time spent staring at a screen isn't good for your mind or your body. If beeps, buzzes, and explosions aren't your cup of tea, try some other fast-paced activity, such as table tennis or badminton.

The master control center for your reactions is, of course, your brain. In a split second it processes information and then sends impulse signals to your muscles. Age brings little change in the speed of these impulses. What slows down is the speed at which information is processed. In other words, slow reactions are due to a sluggish brain, not a sluggish body. So how do you maintain rapid reactions?

Stay mentally and physically fit. Just as giving your body a regular workout increases your strength, balance, and ability to move fast when you need to, when you constantly use your brain and push it to its full capacity, it stays quicker, more alert, and better able to react to new situations.

Get your eyesight checked regularly. Before you can react mentally or physically, you must have an accurate picture of the world outside. For that, you rely on your vision. Regular eye tests are important, not only for checking whether you need glasses or that your lens prescription is up to date, but also spotting eye disorders at an early stage so that they can be treated promptly.

Stop poisoning your brain. Steer clear of tobacco and nonmedicinal drugs and consume alcohol in moderation—or not at all. Everybody knows that drunk drivers are slow to react behind the wheel, but just one or two drinks can be enough to send your reaction times plummeting. If you regularly drink alcohol, it could put your mind and body in a state of constant slow motion. Some medications can reduce your reaction times. If you are concerned about the effect of any medication you are taking, discuss it with your doctor to see if there is an effective alternative available. Tobacco, too, saps your speed in many ways and you can find out why in Part Two: Brain Basics—Seven Steps to a Better Brain.

Stop dithering. Often in life, we are pressed for time. There is no opportunity to do research and you have to make a decision now. Inability to make a decision is a major cause of delayed reaction time. Secret agents go through rigorous training to be mentally prepared to cope with the unexpected. They use that training to make the best possible decision at that moment. You can do the same.

If you are prone to dithering, mentally rehearse how you would respond in certain likely situations so that you are ready to deal with them should they arise. Think about your work or home life and any dilemmas that worry you currently. Now make a list of possible scenarios, both worst case and best case ones. Ask yourself, "What would happen if . . . ?" and, "What would I do then?" Practice making decisions so that if the situation actually occurs, you'll be able to respond with speed and confidence.

Catch some Zzzs. A good night's sleep is nature's way of recharging your mental batteries. Regular, good-quality sleep is essential to keep your brain and body in good shape so that you stay mentally and physically alert and able to react quickly to events. You'll find more information on the brain-boosting qualities of a good night's sleep in Part Two.

Measure your progress so far

Find three soft foam rubber balls and have a go at juggling them. Unless you are an experienced juggler you'll find juggling hard at first, but if you can keep practicing for at least 10 minutes every day, you will begin to notice an improvement. It doesn't matter what system you have for keeping the balls moving and in the air—just keep at it.

Even if you can only juggle for a few seconds before you drop a ball, that's a great start. Studies have shown that learning to juggle has a positive effect on brain function by improving reaction time and boosting intelligence.

Section 7
MIND POWER

he deceptively simple exercises in this section can be repeated over and over again, anytime, anywhere. They are designed to stretch your mind, shake up your everyday routines, use your senses in unusual ways, and by so doing stimulate both sides of your brain.

You don't have to work through this section in any particular order; it's fine just to dip in as you please. For optimum benefits, try to do one or two of the exercises every day—more if you feel up to it. Your brain loves exercise, so if you want to make it happy, give your mind a regular workout. Remember, the more you exercise your brain, the fitter it becomes. Now that you're ready, let's get moving . . .

57 The Mind Dump

Aim: To clear your mind of mental clutter.

Task: On a piece of paper, write down everything that is on your mind right now: your long-term goals, short-term goals, your hopes, your fears, your regrets, what you have to do, any ideas you have, and so on. Writing down what's on your mind has the psychological effect of removing mental clutter. No matter how trivial, just take a snapshot of your thoughts as they are currently by writing them down. Don't go into detail; jot them down in point form—a word or two for each thought will be fine. Keep going until you have nothing left to write. Then take a look at what's on your mind. Do you like what you see?

The Two-Minute Mind

Aim: To learn to focus with a full 100 volts of mental energy.

Task: Find a clock or watch with a second hand and place it directly in front of the television. Switch on the television and try to focus your attention on the movement of the second hand for two whole minutes. Don't allow the television to distract you. If you manage this successfully, make the exercise more challenging by focusing half your attention on the second hand and half your attention on your own hands. Split your focus right down the middle.

59

Creative Tension

Aim: To stay alert for longer.

Task: If you find your mind starts to wander when you are trying to concentrate, try adopting an unfamiliar body posture. For example, change the way you place your legs, alter your facial expression, or tighten your abdominal muscles or leg muscles. If you are with other people, copy someone else's posture. When you put your body in an unfamiliar position like this it stops your body from getting lazy and makes it easier to keep your mind alert.

Mental Gymnastics

Aim: To flex your mental calculating skills.

Task 1: Think of a number and double it. Keep doubling it to see how high you can go. For example: 2, 4, 8, 16, 32, 64 . . .

Task 2: Recite all the numbers from 1 to 100 and . . .

❑ At numbers that can be divided by three, raise your left hand.

❑ At numbers that can be divided by four, raise your right hand.

❑ At numbers that can be divided by three and four, clap your hands.

❑ At numbers that can be divided by five, stamp your feet.

61 Exercise with Letters

Aim: To practice mind drills that encourage mental endurance.

Task 1: Recite the alphabet forward and then backward.

Task 2: Memorize the following verse:

> *Mary had a little lamb*
> *Its fleece was white as snow*
> *Everywhere that Mary went*
> *The lamb was sure to go*

❑ Now recite the verse while also saying the number of letters in each word. For example, Mary (4) had (3) and so on.

❑ Recite the verse line by line backward.

❑ Repeat this exercise with "Humpty Dumpty" and "Jack and Jill."

62

See It with Your Own Eyes

Aim: To make your imagination more vivid.

Task: Close your eyes and visualize each of the following everyday items: a pair of scissors, your house key, a toothbrush, your favorite pair of jeans, your bedroom, your telephone or mobile phone, and a sunset. See them one by one in your mind's eye. Focus first on the shape and then fill in the details. Take your time and allow the image to become steady and sharp.

Now picture in your mind the following imaginary things: a unicorn, a fairy, a chocolate ocean, an ice cream mountain.

What is the difference between your mental images of things you have actually seen and things you have never seen?

63

Mental Music

Aim: To harmonize your thoughts.

Task 1: Play in your "mind's ear" the following well-known pieces of music. Try to "hear" as much as you can:

Classical music: Beethoven's "Moonlight sonata"
Film music: The *Star Wars* soundtrack
Rock music: Queen's "Bohemian Rhapsody"
Pop Music: "Road to Amarillo"

Task 2: Can you mentally hear what the following might sound like:

bright sounds
dark sounds
happy sounds
golden sounds
hollow sounds
rough sounds
smooth sounds?

Now Wash Your Hands

Aim: To stimulate your sensual imagination.

Task: Relax in a comfortable chair and imagine you are washing your hands. Mentally go through every motion and detail. Feel the soap suds, hear the sound of the running water, smell the soap's fragrance, see the bubbles. Now wash your hands for real and compare the experience with what you saw in your mind's eye.

65 Bittersweet

Aim: To activate all your senses.

Task: Give your brain a jolt by imagining the taste and smell of the following foods all mixed together:

Rice pudding and chicken
Milk and orange juice
Pickles and ice cream
Chocolate and mustard

Let the Words Flow

Aim: To improve the way you formulate and express your ideas.

Task 1: Invent meanings for the following nonsense words. When you are finished, why not make up some nonsense words of your own?

Bleesh

Vonderspot

Kagnot

Presstip

Ramplicker

Illustropheno

Task 2: Describe the following as if talking to a Martian: snow, sex, chocolate, how to put on a pair of pants, the Internet, the offside rule in soccer.

Task 3: While holding a conversation, silently repeat to yourself what the other person said before you respond to him or her. This will give you a sense of what that person is really saying. Alternatively (and only if your friends and family work with you on this!), spend a day not talking. Get your messages across using body language and other forms of nonverbal communication only—not notes. For a day, keep yourself free from words.

67 Off the Wall

Aim: To get your mind moving in new directions.

Task: Imagine what it would be like to experience something you cannot perceive directly. For example:

- ❏ What is it like to be a member of the opposite sex?
- ❏ What is it like to be a butterfly?
- ❏ What is it like to be your brain?
- ❏ What is it like to be the first paragraph in a best-selling novel?
- ❏ What is it like to be the Indian Ocean?
- ❏ What is it like to be a tornado?
- ❏ What is it like to be eternity?

68

Strange But True

Aim: To stretch your mind with the paradoxical.

Task: Reflect on the following anecdotes. At first, the sayings below don't seem to make sense, but if you spend time reflecting on them, you may be able to pick up their meaning. The source of these anecdotes is the wise but contrary Mulla Nasrudin, a favorite character in stories throughout the Middle East and Central Asia.

A scholar being ferried by Nasrudin across a body of water chided Nasrudin for his ungrammatical language, and hearing he did not go to school said: "What? Half your life has been wasted!"

Shortly afterward, Nasrudin asked him: "Did you learn to swim?"

"No, I did not," replied the scholar.

"Well, in this case it seems all your life has been wasted . . . we are sinking," said Nasrudin.

Nasrudin is with his cronies drinking coffee. They are discussing death. "When you are in your casket and friends and family are mourning upon you, what would you like to hear them say about you?"

The first crony says, "I would like to hear them say that I was a great doctor of my time, and a great family man."

The second says, "I would like to hear that I was a wonderful husband and school teacher who made a huge difference in our children of tomorrow."

Nasrudin says, "I would like to hear them say . . . look! He's moving!"

A monk said to Mulla Nasrudin, "I am so detached that I never think of myself—only of others." Nasrudin responded, "I am so objective that I can look at myself as if I were another person, so I can afford to think of myself."

Mulla Nasrudin ran into a merchant's tent and asked the owner, "Have you ever seen me before?"

"No, never!" he replied.

"Then how do you know it is me?" Nasrudin cried.

69 Oxymorons

Aim: To stretch the mind by reflecting on words that both puzzle and make sense at the same time.

Task: Oxymorons are a combination of words that when put together seem contradictory or incongruous, such as "Cruel Kindness" or "Jumbo Shrimp." The following expressions are so well known that you may not realize at first that they are oxymorons, but if you roll the words around in your mind for a few moments, you will pick up the often subtle contradictions.

open secret	larger half
clearly confused	act naturally
alone together	Hell's Angels
found missing	liquid gas
rolling stop	deafening silence
seriously funny	living dead
working vacation	freezer burn
jumbo shrimp	advanced Basic
only choice	unbiased opinion
virtual reality	definite maybe
original copies	pretty ugly
same difference	plastic glasses
almost exactly	constant variable
even odds	minor crisis
extinct life	genuine imitation
exact estimate	

70 Brain Teasers

Aim: To develop intuitive thinking.

Task: Take some time to ponder the following questions. Don't try to approach them logically, as they can only be understood intuitively.

- ❏ What is the sound of one hand clapping?
- ❏ What did you look like before you were born?
- ❏ Is the glass half empty or half full?
- ❏ Who are you?
- ❏ If a tree falls in the forest and there is no one around to hear it, does it make a sound?

Measure your progress so far

If you've done at least one of the following today or within the last few days, you are making steady progress with your mental workouts:

- ❏ *Switched off your mobile phone and the television to concentrate on something else.*
- ❏ *Written your thoughts down in a diary or journal.*
- ❏ *Balanced your finances without using a calculator.*
- ❏ *Spoken to someone in person rather than using e-mail.*
- ❏ *Played a board game.*
- ❏ *Read an interesting book or newspaper/magazine feature.*

71 Can You Recall?

Aim: To improve your memory using simple exercises.

Task: Try to recall . . .

- ☐ What you were thinking about five minutes ago.
- ☐ What you were thinking about one hour ago.
- ☐ What you were doing this time yesterday.
- ☐ What you had for breakfast seven days ago.
- ☐ What you wore last weekend.
- ☐ Something you told yourself you would never forget.

72 Empty Your Cup

Aim: To hone right-brained intuitive skills by viewing the world from a new perspective.

Task: Read the following story. What can you learn from it?

A student visited a Zen master to ask him about Zen. As is the custom, the master served tea. He poured the student's cup to the brim and then kept on pouring. The student looked on in astonishment as the tea overflowed. Finally he said, "The cup is full. No more will go in." The master stopped pouring, looked at the student, smiled, and said, "Like this cup, you are full of your own ideas and opinions and speculations. How can I teach you until you empty your cup?"

73 Vital Learning

Aim: To understand the meaning of wisdom.

Task: Answer the following:

❏ What five things that you have learned in your life would you want to pass down to your grandchildren?

❏ List five questions that everyone should be able to answer if they want to be considered a wise human being.

74

Measuring Up

Aim: To test observational skills and spatial awareness.

Task: Using paper and a pencil, draw the following without measuring them:

❑ A standard first-class postage stamp.
❑ A line as long as your foot.
❑ A circle the same size as a quarter.
❑ A rectangle the same size as your mobile phone.
❑ A rectangle the same size as your credit card.

Now compare your drawings with the actual objects to see how observant you are and how accurately you perceive the world. If they were way off the mark, you need to sharpen your observational skills and take time to notice the tiny details of your life.

75

Try Something New

Aim: To stretch the mind by making familiar experiences unfamiliar.

Task: Clasp your hands with fingers interlaced. See which thumb is on top, the right or the left. Try clasping your hands a different way. Now fold your arms and notice which arm is on top, right or left. Try folding them the other way.

List five other things you do every day in exactly the same way, such as crossing your legs or sitting on the same sofa seat. Think about how you can do these things differently.

76 Stop Looking Back

Aim: To break free of regressive thought patterns.

Task: For one day, monitor your thoughts and notice how often you think about past events. We spend a lot of our time living in the past, yet the brain craves new ideas and different experiences. An antidote to regressive thinking is to do a mind power exercise for five or ten minutes every day.

77 Backward Spelling

Aim: To develop clarity of thinking using simple mind-stretching techniques.

Task 1: Choose a book or a newspaper and select five four-letter words, five five-letter words, and five six-letter words. Beginning with the four-letter words, glance at the first word, then turn away and spell it backward out loud. Do this for each word in your list. If you find this easy, try seven-, eight-, nine-, or ten-letter words. If you managed to do this task, try the next one.

Task 2: At the end of the day, just before you go to bed, try to remember the events of your day, only working backward. In other words, start with this evening's events and work back to the moment when you woke up this morning.

78

Opposite Directions

Aim: To improve hand–eye coordination.

Task 1: Pat your stomach with your right hand and make an imaginary circle above your head with your left hand. Now swap hands. You will find one way more difficult than the other. Keep practicing until you find both ways easy. When you've mastered this, here's something else your brain will love.

Task 2: While sitting at your desk, make clockwise circles with your right foot. (Go ahead, no one will see you!) While you're doing this, draw the figure 6 in the air with your right hand. Your foot will start circling in a counterclockwise direction. Keep practicing until you can stop your foot from changing direction.

79 Two Sides to Every Story

Aim: To view yourself in a completely different light.

Task: Take a sheet of paper and a pencil and list six words that describe you: the qualities that make you the person you think you are. Now take another sheet of paper and write six more words that you also feel describe yourself, but this time use your other hand to write. You'll find this tricky and clumsy at first. When you have finished, compare both lists. In most cases the words in the first list will be longer and more impersonal and the words in the second list more emotional and imaginative. This is because the first list came from your left brain and the second list came from your right brain. It's easier to learn when both sides of your brain are activated. Take a look at your list again and see how the qualities in the first list can be softened and balanced by the qualities in the second and vice versa.

80

On the Other Hand

Aim: Improve manual dexterity by using your non-dominant hand.

Task: Try the following, using your left hand if you are right-handed or your right hand if you are left-handed:

- ❏ Brush your teeth.
- ❏ Pick up a glass, mug, or cup and drink from it.
- ❏ Comb your hair.
- ❏ Write a short note or shopping list.
- ❏ Get dressed (using only your nondominant hand).
- ❏ Eat a meal (with knife and fork in opposite hands).

Really Seeing

Aim: To sharpen your observational skills.

Task: Take a sheet of paper and a pen or pencil and list every object that you see around you, big and small. You'll need lots of time for this. Use your eyes to really see.

Even Handed

Aim: To become ambidextrous by using both hands and both parts of your brain at the same time.

Task 1: Take a piece of paper and a pencil. Pick up the pencil in both hands and write your name, using both hands at the same time.

Task 2: Take a second pencil and write your first name with your left hand and your last name with your right hand, again at the same time.

Task 3: Hold the paper against your forehead and write your last name with your left hand if you are right-handed or your first name with your right hand if you are left-handed.

The results may surprise you!

83

Sudoku Time

Aim: Let logic alone be your guide!

Task: Every column, every row, and every 3x3 mini-grid must be filled in with the numbers from 1 to 9.

								3
	7	2	1				9	
			5	8			4	7
	3	1			9	6	7	4
		7		2		3		
5	9	6	4			8	1	
9	6			7	5			
	5				4	9	6	
1								

(Answer on page 227.)

84

Say It Out Loud

Aim: To stimulate your brain by reading out loud.

You use different parts of your brain when you are reading aloud and when you are reading silently. You may find that hearing the words as well as seeing them makes a big difference to your understanding.

Task: The next time you open an e-mail or a letter, instead of reading it silently, say it out loud and see if this alters the meaning in any way.

Master Brain

Aim: To discover new ways to expand your knowledge.

Task: Learn how to spell "brain" in French, German, Italian, Spanish, Dutch, and as many other languages as you can find. Here's five to get you going:

French: *Cerveau*

German: *Gehirn*

Italian: *Cervello*

Spanish: *Cerebro*

Dutch: *Brein*

Measure your progress so far

If you have done at least one of the following today or in the last few days, you are increasing your brain power.

❑ *Taken a different route to work.*

❑ *Brushed your teeth using your nondominant hand.*

❑ *Switched your watch to the other wrist.*

❑ *Worn a color you never normally wear.*

❑ *Thought about what you want to achieve tomorrow.*

86 Close Your Eyes

Aim: To stimulate and enhance your perception of touch.

Task: In the morning, try to get dressed with your eyes closed. Keep your eyes closed and feel your way around using your sense of touch and your spatial memory alone. Take your time dressing. To avoid bumping your head on closet doors, prepare the night before by laying your clothes out ready for the morning. Closing your eyes gives your brain an opportunity to create new associations. Notice the feel of the clothes, and concentrate on all the other senses that are diminished when you have your eyes open.

87 Get Lost

Aim: To broaden your mind with the unfamiliar.

Task: Take a different route today, for example, to your workplace, the grocery store, school, or when visiting a friend or relative. It doesn't matter whether you are walking or driving, the important thing is that you try something new. Unfamiliar sights, sounds, and smells stimulate all your senses. If you get lost along the way, all the better. You are using spatial awareness to get you back in the right direction.

Word Ladders

Aim: Challenge the part of your brain that deals with language.

Task: Fill in the step of each "ladder" below with a word, changing one letter as you climb so that you end up with the final word. Each step on the ladder must be a valid word. For example, "Turn Calm into Rage" = CALM, palm, pale, page, RAGE. This type of puzzle was invented in 1878 by Lewis Carroll, the author of *Alice in Wonderland*.

Turn Smile into Tears:

SMILE ____ ____ ____ ____ ____ TEARS

Turn Nail into File:

NAIL ____ ____ ____ FILE

Turn Give into Take:

GIVE ____ ____ ____ TAKE

Turn Navy into Army:

NAVY ____ ____ ____ ____ ____ ____ ____ ARMY

(Answers on page 227.)

89

Work Experience

Aim: To expand your mental horizons by seeing your world through someone else's eyes.

Task: Invite someone new into your home or workplace for a couple of hours. (You may need to clear it with your boss and colleagues first.) The simple act of explaining your lifestyle or way of working to others will do wonders for your people skills. You'll also get a fresh perspective on everything that you have taken for granted in your daily life.

90

Elementary Logic

Aim: Pure logic needs to be applied here. Don't be distracted by reality or personal opinion.

Task: By looking at the statements below, can you make reasonable conclusions in each case as shown by the following example? "All dogs understand Spanish. Some cats are dogs." Conclusion: Some cats understand Spanish. It's perfectly reasonable if you let logic alone be your guide that cats may be dogs and either animal can understand Spanish.

1) All ice skaters can dance.
Some dancers are rugby players.
Conclusion:

2) All lawyers are people we trust.
All lawyers are liars.
Conclusion:

3) All successful businesspeople are teetotalers.
All young businesspeople are heavy drinkers.
Conclusion:

(Answers on page 227.)

Keep It in the Family

Aim: Nothing clever here; you just need to think logically.

Task: What is the smallest group of relatives that could contain all of the following family relationships: aunt, brother, cousin, daughter, mother, nephew, niece, sister, uncle, father, and son? (Answer on page 227.)

92

Focus on Food

Aim: To enhance your sensory perception of food.

Task: Eat in silence. There must be no TV, no chatter, and no distractions. Simply focus on the taste, smell, and texture of the food you are eating. Freed from all other distractions, your mind is able to give its full attention to the four well-known taste sensations: salty, sweet, sour, and bitter. You might even try holding your nose occasionally, as this puts your sense of taste center stage. With the sense of smell blocked, you can't recognize flavor, and this allows you to focus on other sensations, such as mouthfeel, temperature, texture, and crunchiness.

Switch Seats

Aim: To change your mental perspective by changing your physical view.

Task: Sit in a different seat at dinner time or when watching television. If you share your home with others, you may encounter some resistance at first, as most people have favorite seats, but they may all gain something from the novelty of the experience. Switching seats forces you to change your view of the room, the position you occupy in it, and how you interact with other people. Simply changing seats will challenge and rework old, established mental associations and add a spark to your thought processes.

94

Exercise Outdoors

Aim: To give both brain and body a workout at the same time.

Task: Take some exercise out in the open. You could start with a few simple exercises in the garden, such as skipping, jogging in place, or jumping jacks. Then try walking, jogging, running, or cycling in a nearby park or recreational area. Outdoor exercising stimulates the blood circulation and so improves the flow of oxygen and nutrients to the brain, and the novel multisensory experience will stimulate the development of new neural pathways in the brain. Even if you exercise regularly in a gym, you will benefit by breaking your routine every now and again and exercising outdoors instead. Your brain thrives on novelty and unpredictability.

Upside Down!

Aim: Strengthen your brain by encouraging it to make sense of the unfamiliar.

Task: Wear your watch upside down or on the opposite wrist. You could also try reading upside down. Start with a few sentences, and gradually move on to whole paragraphs as you become more adept.

96

Listen While You Work

Aim: To expand the mind and make more use of leisure and commuting time.

Task: Listen to audio books whenever you have spare listening time. There are many occasions when you are doing tasks that do not take up all your attention. They include commuting by bus, train, or car (especially when stuck in traffic jams!), or when doing household chores or DIY. A good way to use this spare time productively, and learn something new, is to listen to audio books. You can find a wide selection of titles—both fiction and non-fiction, on tape or compact disc—at public libraries, in bookstores, or via online suppliers.

97

Sit Up Straight

Aim: To improve posture and brain power at the same time.

Task: Sit up straight, and hold that position. Good posture affects your state of mind, and helps you think more clearly. Try the following experiment and prove this to yourself.

Recite the 13 times table in your head, first while slouching, with your mouth open, then while sitting up straight, with your lips together. You'll get the point.

98

Did You Know?

Aim: To encourage your curiosity.

Task: Ponder the following:

- ❑ Shakespeare invented the words "assassination" and "bump."
- ❑ Cows and horses sleep standing up.
- ❑ If you get the recommended eight hours' sleep every night, it means you are asleep for four months each year.
- ❑ Flying fish do not actually fly; instead, they glide over the water.
- ❑ There are eight species of bear in the world.
- ❑ There are more than 500 active volcanoes in the world.
- ❑ More people collect stamps than any other item.
- ❑ In the China Sea and western Pacific, hurricanes are known as typhoons.
- ❑ In some parts of Argentina they speak Welsh.
- ❑ The word "coffee" was once a term for wine.
- ❑ The geographical heart of Europe is Lithuania.
- ❑ The Austrians invented the croissant.
- ❑ Dolphins are the only other mammals besides humans that have sex for fun.

Get Word Savvy

Aim: To build your vocabulary.

Task: Look up a new word in the dictionary every day and learn it. Say it out loud and then use it in a sentence. A good starting point is to sign up to the "Word of the Day" online at www.yourdictionary.com. Playing Scrabble regularly or doing a daily crossword works well too.

Box Clever

Aim: To make watching television more challenging for the brain.

Too much television turns your brain to mush. The typical adult watches around 28 hours of TV per week. Count up the amount of time you spend watching television, and if it averages out at more than one or two hours a day, find ways to cut down. The following task can help you get the most out of the time you do spend in front of the TV.

Task: Try out some of the ideas below:

❑ Play a challenging board game or play along with a TV game that tests your mental powers.

❑ When listening to an interview, take note of the number of times the interviewee says "umm."

❑ If you hear an unfamiliar word, look it up in the dictionary.

❑ During the commercial break, try to think up new names for all the products.

❑ Watch the news and when it is over try to recall all the topics that were covered.

101

Audio Visual

Aim: To exercise both brain hemispheres and create new neural connections by reading aloud.

Task: Read aloud. Just a minute or so a day spent reading aloud will benefit the brain. The tougher the title the better. (Think Emily Brontë's *Wuthering Heights*, Jane Austen's *Pride and Prejudice*, or Charles Dickens's *Bleak House*.) For best results, speak clearly and quickly. Of course, silent reading helps improve brain function, too, so read as much as you can about as wide a range of subjects as possible. Books exercise your brain, provide inspiration, and fill you with information that allows you to make creative connections more easily.

Measure your progress so far

If you have done at least one of the following today, or over the last few days, you are making your brain happy. Try to keep it that way.

❑ *Attempted two of the exercises in this book.*
❑ *Played a game of chess.*
❑ *Finished a crossword puzzle.*
❑ *Made the most out of your Web surfing by going to a site such as www.wikipedia.com and searching for any topic that interests you.*
❑ *Changed a routine.*
❑ *Taken up a new hobby.*
❑ *Disagreed with someone without losing your temper.*
❑ *Remembered a dream that you had the previous night.*
❑ *Learned something new.*
❑ *Imagined the impossible.*

2

Brain Basics
Seven Steps to
a Better Brain

Step 1
FOOD FOR THOUGHT

You are what you eat, and that includes your brain, of course. Food powers your body and fuels your brain, so whatever you eat and drink will affect your physical and mental well-being in some way. If you don't eat properly, your brain can begin to function less efficiently, resulting in foggy thinking, poor concentration, and forgetfulness.

Your brain is an amazing instrument of cognition (thinking), emotion, and intuition. It's also the greediest organ in your body, requiring a constant supply of glucose energy, oxygen, and other nutrients. So what is the ultimate Super Brain diet?

What every brain needs

Even if your diet has been less than optimum in the past, it's never too late to boost your brain power with healthy eating. Above all, your brain needs glucose, but the supply needs to be a steady one. That means eating starchy carbohydrates such as bread, pasta, rice, and potatoes that release glucose energy into the bloodstream at a constant rate. Simple sugars, from candy, cake, cookies, and chocolate, release too much energy too quickly, resulting in an energy surge (a sugar "high"), making you feel hyperactive. This is rapidly followed by an energy slump, leaving you feeling tired and lethargic. Skipping meals is a bad idea, too, because if there's too little glucose energy in your bloodstream, you'll feel sluggish and find it hard to concentrate.

If you want to avoid stressing your brain with too much or too little sugar, make sure you always eat breakfast. Many studies have shown that breakfast is good news if you want to keep your brain active and functioning efficiently. Your brain never rests, even when you are asleep (think how active it must be during your dreams!). So that energy needs to be replaced when you wake up. Eating breakfast is the best way to replenish fuel stores and prevent mental meltdown later in the morning.

So, breakfast has got you off to a good start. Now you have to maintain your energy levels throughout the day. The best way to do this is to eat six small, balanced, nutritious meals spread throughout the day, and make sure each of them contains some high-quality protein and a little unsaturated fat—a sprinkling of nuts and seeds, for example. By eating little and often you consume less overall yet keep your blood sugar on an even keel. That is better than having two or three large meals a day, which can lead to big energy swings and excess intake of calories.

But it isn't just a matter of getting a steady intake of energy every couple of hours. For optimal brain function you also need to pay attention to the types of foods you are actually putting into your mouth.

Fasting

In most religions around the world, periods of fasting or cutting down on food are intrinsically a part of the religious calendar. Last year I fasted for a short period of time at a health clinic and was amazed to find I wasn't at all hungry but, more interestingly, how my mind seemed to be freeing itself.

Over a matter of days I was able to cope with business problems and deeper decisions that I had been struggling with for many months. Somehow it was like fasting had broken down shackles inside my head. I loved the sensation. It became searingly obvious to me that fasting had been introduced into religions for precisely this clarity of mind, so that faith may be followed more resolutely. What a powerful natural tool.

How to feed your brain

In general, you are better off eating carbohydrates that are fresh and unprocessed, such as vegetables, fruits, whole grains, whole wheat pasta, brown rice, nuts, seeds, and pulses (beans and peas), rather than heavily processed foods such as white bread, white rice, fries, and prepackaged meals. This is because fresh, unprocessed foods are broken down in the body at a steady rate, thereby giving your brain a steady supply of sugar. They also contain the all-important vitamins, minerals, and other nutrients so often lost during processing. Aim for one third of your daily food intake to be made up of unprocessed, starchy carbohydrates.

Proteins are important, too. They provide the building blocks called amino acids that are needed to maintain and repair all the body's tissues, including the brain. In particular, they provide the essential amino acids, including tryptophan, from which brain chemicals, or neurotransmitters, such as serotonin are made. Protein foods also help control the release of sugar into your bloodstream. To ensure that you obtain the full range of essential amino acids you need, try to include a wide range of quality protein in your diet, in the form of low-fat cheese, low-fat milk, low-fat yogurt, lean meat and poultry, fish, eggs, soy products (such as tofu), lentils, whole grain cereals, nuts, and seeds.

If you prefer not to eat animal sources of protein, such as meat, fish, and eggs, you can still get all the essential amino acids you need from plant-based foods. But you must make sure that you eat the widest possible range of vegetable protein sources, including peas, beans, lentils, grains, nuts, and seeds. Other good sources of vegetable protein include quinoa, soy products, buckwheat, millet, and wild rice.

When it comes to dairy and meat products, always opt for lean/low-fat products and limit your intake of saturated fats, found in red meat, full-fat dairy products, and refined, processed foods high in palm oil. Don't cut out fats and oils altogether, though, because your brain cells and other cells of the nervous system, including the retina in the eye, require very specialized types, in particular, long-chain omega-3 essential fatty acids, found in oily fish, such as sardines and mackerel, as well as walnuts and green leafy vegetables.

Brain-boosting vitamins and minerals

B vitamins are brain vitamins. Most B vitamins, including folic acid, and some minerals, are essential for nerve cells and a healthy brain. In particular, they are needed for the repair and maintenance of neurons and nerve connections, for creating nerve signals, and for the production of neurotransmitters. Here are the key players:

❑ *Vitamin B_1 (thiamine) is contained in whole grains and enriched grain products such as whole grain bread, rice, pasta, and fortified cereals, as well as fresh and dried fruit, milk, cheese, eggs, and pork.*

❑ *Vitamin B_5 (pantothenic acid) is in lean meat, poultry, eggs, whole grain cereals, pulses, broccoli, tomatoes, and fruit.*

❑ *Vitamin B_6 (pyridoxine) can be found in chicken, fish, pork, liver, kidney, and eggs, as well as whole grain cereals, nuts, and legumes.*

❑ *Vitamin B_{12} (cobalamin) is in eggs, meat, fish, poultry, and low-fat dairy products.*

❑ *Folic acid, or folate (also known as vitamin B_9) is found in bananas, orange juice, fortified cereals, lemons, strawberries, cantaloupe, leafy vegetables, dried beans, and peas.*

❑ *Iron is found in lean beef, whole grain breads, raisins, dried apricots, legumes, and low-fat bran muffins. (Iron deficiency is especially common in women due to the loss of blood during menstruation and can result in tiredness, poor concentration, and lethargy.)*

❏ *Calcium is in leafy green vegetables, low-fat dairy products, soy products, fish with bones (such as sardines), nuts, and seeds. (Women on a quest to avoid the fat in calcium-enriched dairy products are often deficient in this crucial mineral.)*

❏ *Magnesium is found in whole grains, legumes, nuts, and green vegetables.*

❏ *Potassium is found in apricots, avocados, bananas, grapefruit, kiwi, oranges, prunes, strawberries, potatoes, lean meat, and fish.*

❏ *Zinc is found in beans and lentils, yeast, nuts, seeds, and whole grain cereals.*

Water is vital for a healthy brain. That's why you get headaches and can't concentrate properly if you are dehydrated. The solution: make sure you drink around eight glasses of fluids a day to stay hydrated—more on hot days or if you have been exercising. Pure water is the best drink to have. One way to ensure you are drinking enough is to fill a pitcher or bottle with your targeted amount and drink it throughout the day. If the container is empty by bedtime, you'll know you have achieved your goal. Don't wait until you are thirsty to drink, as thirst is a sign that you are already becoming dehydrated.

A-grade antioxidants—brain protectors

Antioxidants are substances found in food that help protect the brain and so help maintain healthy brain function, including memory. In particular, antioxidants neutralize free radicals, the highly damaging molecules produced naturally in the body and also generated by smoking, pollution, and sunlight, that can otherwise attack neurons and other nerve cells.

So it's worth making sure you are getting enough A-grade antioxidants in your diet. Ideally, fruit and vegetables should make up one third of your total food intake each day. If so, and you are eating at least the recommended five different types of vegetables and fruit a day, as well as whole grains and other fresh food, your antioxidant intake is likely to be high. The following are good sources of antioxidants:

❑ *Beta carotene* is found in orange and yellow fruits and vegetables such as carrots and pumpkins. Getting enough beta carotene means eating a well-rounded diet, according to the guidelines in this chapter, with lots of fruits and vegetables. Brightly colored fruits and vegetables have especially high levels of beta carotene. They include: sweet potato, carrots, green vegetables, apricots, bell peppers, corn, broccoli, mango, and squash.

❑ *Vitamin C* is found in citrus fruits, such as oranges, and in strawberries, raspberries, blackberries, sweet potatoes, green and red peppers, and green leafy vegetables, such as broccoli and cauliflower. If you make sure you eat at least five servings of brightly colored fruits and vegetables a day, you should be getting sufficient vitamin C.

❑ *Vitamin E* is found in nuts, seeds, vegetable oils, whole grains, and oily fish. If you are eating plenty of whole grains every day and snacking between meals on a handful of nuts and seeds, your vitamin E intake should be fine.

❑ *Selenium* is found in Brazil nuts, cereals, seafood, and eggs. If you include some whole grains, fish and/or Brazil nuts daily, you should be able to get all the selenium you need from your diet.

❑ *Zinc* is found in fish, legumes, and almonds. Most people can get enough zinc in their diet by eating a variety of foods each day, including lean meat, fish, and poultry. Vegetarians can get zinc when they eat legumes such as fresh and dried peas and beans, soy products, lentils, and chickpeas (used to make hummus).

Digestive health

Keeping regular by maintaining healthy bowel function is important, too. Sluggish digestive transit can lead to headaches, fatigue, and low libido. That's why fiber should be nominated as the unsung brain food hero! If you are eating at least five servings of fruits and vegetables a day, you are well on your way toward your optimal fiber intake. You can get the rest from high-fiber foods such as whole grain cereals, nuts, and seeds.

Top 10 brain foods

The following foods not only make a delicious addition to any diet, they are also packed with nutrients that are especially "brain friendly."

❑ *Blueberries are bursting with antioxidants and phytochemicals (plant nutrients) that help sharpen your brain.*

❑ *Leafy greens, such as spinach and broccoli, contain folic acid and vitamin B_6, which help convert tryptophan into serotonin, a brain chemical that boosts your mood and alertness and also plays a role in controlling sleep cycles.*

❑ *Oily fish are full of omega-3 fatty acids for healthy brain cells and nerves, so Grandma was right—oily fish is brain food. Good sources are the cold water fish, mackerel, salmon, herrings, and sardines. Good sources of omega-3 for vegetarians include pumpkin seeds and walnuts.*

❑ *Grape juice is rich in brain-protecting antioxidants, making it the smarter beverage choice.*

❑ *Brown rice, like all whole grain foods, is one of the best things you can eat to improve your intake of brain-boosting nutrients. It's packed with the protein, vitamins, and minerals your brain loves.*

❑ *Cranberries are not only tasty berries but also bursting with antioxidants, which means they are particularly good for the brain.*

❑ *Turmeric, the spice that gives curry its yellow color and distinctive flavor, is high in antioxidants and can help protect the brain against mental decline.*

❑ *Olive oil is rich in vitamin E, an important antioxidant for healthy brain function. The extra-virgin variety is best because the oil is produced naturally, without chemical treatment.*

❑ *Garlic is a powerful antioxidant that can also help shake off stress-induced colds and infections. Raw, crushed garlic is best. Cooked garlic is less powerful but still enhances blood circulation in the brain.*

❑ *Cocoa is well known as a great bedtime drink that helps you get all the sleep you need to recharge your brain. Now it seems cocoa can help your brain in other ways, too. Research has shown that there is almost twice as much antioxidant content in two tablespoons of pure cocoa powder as in the equivalent amount of red wine, up to three times more than green tea, and four to five times more than black tea.*

Brain bandits

Just as some foods are brain boosters, other foods can rob the brain of healthy brain function and even cause lasting damage.

See-sawing sugary foods

Sucrose (table sugar) and fructose, and processed flour products, found in cookies, cake, candy, sauces, and fast foods, cause wild fluctuations in blood sugar. They leave you feeling fidgety, irritable, inattentive, and even sleepy— not an ideal state for efficient brain function. Excess consumption of sugar and processed flour have also been implicated in diabetes, obesity, heart disease, and cancer, so it makes sense to cut back on them as much as possible.

Blood blockers

Trans fatty acids and saturated fats, found in foods such as cookies, potato chips, fries, and pastries, and full-fat dairy and fatty meat products, can clog your arteries and disrupt the flow of blood, oxygen, and nutrients to the brain. They are also implicated in type 2 diabetes and obesity, and so it is smart to consume saturated fats in moderation only—and avoid trans fats altogether.

Silent assassins

Although the odd glass or two won't hurt, and may actually benefit your brain, too much alcohol can destroy brain cells, so if you want to stay mentally sharp, limit your intake to one, possibly two glasses of wine, beer, or spirits a day tops. (It's also smart to give your body a break of one or two days at least once a month so that your liver and brain get a chance to recover.) Nicotine causes constriction of blood vessels, which restricts blood flow to your brain, so smoking isn't advised if you want to boost your brain power. Too much salt (sodium) isn't good news either, as it increases the risk of high blood pressure. As far as caffeine is concerned, one or two cups of coffee a day seems to have a stimulating effect on your brain, but if you drink more than that, you are asking for trouble as it decreases blood flow to your brain significantly.

Toxic terrors

It's also a good idea to avoid as many man-made chemicals as possible. Research suggests that many chemicals commonly used in food (i.e., additives such as coloring, flavoring, and preservatives), in your house (cleaning products), and garden (pesticides and herbicides) can hinder optimum brain function. If you want to increase your brain power, you should be smart enough to opt for natural, preferably organic, food and limit the amount of chemicals you use in the garden and home.

Supplements

Dietitians believe that, in most cases, if you eat a balanced diet, you shouldn't need supplements, but it's sometimes tricky to maintain perfect balance in your meals. Women of childbearing age are advised to take a folic acid supplement, and elderly people certainly benefit from supplements. As an insurance policy, I think it is a good idea for most people to take a comprehensive multivitamin and mineral supplement. Studies suggest the brain can benefit from long-term vitamin and mineral supplementation.

If you can't manage to eat oily fish twice a week, then supplementing with a

Warning: If you are receiving prescription medication, always check with your doctor or pharmacist before taking herbal supplements. Some herbal supplements can interfere with medications, either reducing their effectiveness or causing serious side effects.

good-quality fish oil that is high in omega-3 fatty acids will ensure a steady and adequate supply for your ever-hungry brain. We all take fish oil supplements in our house. I've seen the difference it has had on my young children and have now read the scientific research conducted around the world showing the benefits of a daily intake of fish oils on young minds.

When it comes to herbal supplements, ginkgo biloba stands head and shoulders above the rest. More evidence exists for the beneficial effect of ginkgo on mental function than for any other herb. It is said to improve memory, boost concentration, and sharpen mental focus in people of all ages. As with all supplements, follow the instructions on the packet and never exceed the stated dose.

The 10 golden rules of smart eating

❑ *Eat breakfast every day.*

❑ *Don't leave more than three hours between meals or snacks.*

❑ *Eat quality protein with each meal.*

❑ *Make sure one third of your diet is fruits and vegetables.*

❑ *Eat at least five different types of fruits and vegetables a day.*

❑ *Eat oily fish two or three times a week.*

❑ *Make sure one third of your diet is starchy foods.*

❑ *Go for whole grains and fresh, preferably organic, foods.*

❑ *Drink enough water to keep yourself fully hydrated.*

❑ *Enjoy the odd glass of red wine, cup of coffee, or bar of chocolate.*

Step 2
MEMORY MARVELS

mind like a sieve? Don't worry, there is a lot more to memory than just remembering and a lot you can do to boost your memory. Many people assume that forgetfulness and mental decline are an inevitable part of aging, but this isn't the case. Memory lapses can occur at any age. You just start noticing them (and worrying about them) more when you're older.

Children are incredibly forgetful and so are young adults—take a look at the lost-and-found counter at any busy railway station or airport. Your memory is probably a lot better than you think it is, and with a little training you have the ability to make it sharper—and keep it that way. Whether you are young or old, the more you use your brain the better it works. You are never too old to learn and relearn, and that can happen at any stage of life, even into old age. Exercising your brain is the key to keeping your memory intact.

IQ tests—handle with care

An intelligence test is designed to test your mental ability. An IQ—or intelligence quotient—is a number said to express relative intelligence. It is determined by dividing your mental age (as reflected by your performance on a standardized test) by your chronological age and multiplying by 100. An example of the formula is as follows. You are 20 years old and a standardized IQ test of your logic and reasoning ability puts your mental age at the higher level of 25. Your IQ would be your mental age, 25, divided by your real age, 20, multiplied by 100, which makes 125.

If you take another IQ test and this time score 130, this doesn't mean you have become smarter; it simply means you performed better on that particular test. So an intelligence test measures your performance on that one test alone, and your performance on one test is a poor guide to your true intelligence. Bear in mind, too, that there are many kinds of intelligence. Some people consider emotional intelligence to be just as important, if not more so, than logic and reasoning in predicting success and happiness in life. So, the message is don't get hung up on your IQ—if you know it—but rather focus on how to use your brain effectively and what you want to accomplish with it.

Introducing your working memory

Until recently, your mental problem-solving ability, as measured by IQ tests, was thought to be fixed and impossible to change. Exciting new research, however, shows that there is a very basic brain function called working memory (just like you find in a computer). It is thought that working memory is the foundation of your problem-solving ability, and this opens up the intriguing possibility that if your working memory can be trained and improved, you can boost your IQ too.

For an example of working memory, consider the following. Imagine you get lost while looking for a town center parking lot. You stop at a service station and the attendant says, "Take a left turn at the first traffic circle. Go for about three miles until you see a set of traffic lights and turn right into Blake Street. Then go for about one mile and you'll see the parking lot on your left."

Even as you read this, you may be imagining repeating the directions over and over, under your breath, as you drive to your destination. The type of memory needed to hold such temporary information in your mind while problem solving is called working memory.

The amount of information that your working memory can hold is thought to be strongly related to your general intelligence and IQ rating. Although we use our working memory all the time to solve problems, most of us don't use it efficiently. Research has shown, however, that there are techniques you can use to train your working memory, giving results that are both impressive and immediate.

Something to jog your memory

Picture this: You are introduced to a class of 30 children. They all sit in a circle and each child tells you their name.

188 · SUPER BRAIN

Thirty minutes later you are asked to remember their names. Could you do it?

Most of us would struggle hopelessly at this, and yet each one of us is probably up to the task. It just needs a little strategy and practice. Many memory strategies, such as acronyms or using melody or rhyme, are based on the technique called mnemonics. This is the principle of associating something complex with something more familiar. If you have worked through the exercises in Part One, you will already have seen several examples of mnemonics. The trick is to make the association as vivid as possible.

Practice makes perfect

It's very clear that the more you practice something physically, say learning to drive a manual car, the easier it will become. We all know this is true physically, but it is also true mentally. The ways in which our brains can improve and the speed at which they can generate new pathways is astonishing.

Practicing with numbers still helps me enormously when we record Countdown. *We make the TV shows in batches of 10 programs over 2-day periods (5 shows a day). Sometimes we don't go back into the studio for many weeks after a summer break. At that point I find I'm a bit rusty at the numbers game, so during the morning and while the letters games are in progress, I practice about 100 numbers games to get my speed back up to what it should be, and then I'm raring to go.*

So, in this case, practice doesn't just make perfect, it helps me to keep my job!

"Chunking"—breaking information into chunks—is a technique often used to remember numbers, although it can be used for remembering other things as well. It is based on the idea that most people can remember a maximum of between five and nine things at one time. U.S. telephone numbers, without the area code, contain seven digits. This is convenient because it is the average amount of numbers that a person can keep in his or her mind at one time. Now that all numbers require you to also dial the area code, it helps to break the longer number into chunks. So, a number that includes the digits 2324459612 can be better remembered as 232–445–9612.

Visualization can be used as a memory aid. It involves creating a mental image, preferably a ridiculous one, that sticks in your mind. For example, you are going to the supermarket to buy groceries and you need to remember bread, eggs, flour, and orange juice. One way to recall your shopping list is to picture a loaf of bread breaking open with eggs and orange juice spilling out into a bowl of flour. The image is absurd but helps you to remember the individual items.

Try to add smells and sounds to your visual imagery. We normally gather information using all our senses, and so it is more effective if you can use them all to help you remember. Smell scrambled eggs on toast, for example, or taste the tang of orange juice. Recall the silky sticky feel of flour when it is wet.

Another technique is to "read it and say it." When trying to remember written text, it often helps to say the words aloud, as hearing the information helps you retain it. For example, if you are given written instructions or directions, try repeating them to yourself aloud. One theory about why this works is that your right brain is used for visual memory and your left for verbal memory, so by both looking at and hearing the instructions your whole brain is being used to remember them.

Tried-and-trusted memory boosters

If you have done all you can to remember things, but your life is so busy that you still find yourself, for example, forgetting where you put your car keys or your glasses, try the following tried-and-trusted tips.

❑ *Write it down. Carry a pen and paper with you at all times and if you need to remember something important, write it down immediately. Sticky notes are great for posting notes on your fridge, computer, and phone. Or you could phone home and leave a message on your answering machine.*

❑ *Make a mental image. When you put your mobile phone down, or place your keys in a drawer for safe keeping, allow yourself a few moments to make a mental image of the place you left them. It also helps to leave your keys and mobile phone in the same place each time. As an additional safeguard, have copies made of your keys and leave a set with someone you can trust.*

❑ *Numbers. With so many passwords to remember today for banks, and to use the computer, it might help to have the same number for all of them. If you are worried that your security may be compromised by just having one number, use some of the mnemonics techniques mentioned above and in Part One to remember them.*

❑ *Make a list. If you are the kind of person who worries about whether or not you have turned off the lights or the oven or fed the fish, make a list that you can put beside—or attach to—your exit door, and before you leave simply scan the list to make sure you have remembered everything and give yourself peace of mind.*

❑ *Save the best to last. We tend to remember the tasks we find most interesting and to forget the routine and boring tasks. So try to do the mundane things first—or better still right away—so that you are less likely to forget to do them, and save the interesting tasks for the end.*

If you want to improve your memory (and your ability to learn), you need to exercise it, exercise it, and exercise it more. Working through the exercises in this book will give you all the training you need to brush the cobwebs from your mental book shelves, challenge your brain, and refresh your memory.

Step 3
THE
MOZART
EFFECT

music may tune up your thinking, but is it possible to crank up the volume and become a genius? Ever since research first suggested that something as simple as listening to Mozart could boost children's brain power, educators all over the world have linked music making with better language skills, math ability, improved school results, and improvements in problem solving.

The Mozart theory has also captured the imagination of the public. Some parents have been snapping up every available copy of the maestro's work. Nursery schools have been dutifully playing it to their charges, and some states have even been sending free Mozart CDs to families with a new baby. The Mozart effect has stimulated an industry! But is there a link between intelligence and music?

Why music?

What is it about Mozart that seems to jumpstart the brain, especially when it comes to math-related subjects? Experts say it may be because music never stands still. Whether you are playing an instrument or listening to the radio, your brain is constantly being challenged to process and make sense of the tune and rhythm. Music is also thought to stimulate areas of your brain used for other skills, such as math, reading, and problem solving.

Another reason why Mozart is considered so special is that his music appears to activate both the left and right brain. In most of us, the left side of the brain is the logical, rational side of the brain. It deals with letters, numbers, language, facts, diagrams, dates, and technical information. The right side of the brain deals with creativity, imagery, color, and imagination. The left brain recognizes names. The right brain recognizes faces. Activities that use both sides at the same time are thought to engage the brain's full capacity, and it is this that boosts thinking skills and intelligence.

Tuning up

It seems that music lessons might be the key to unlocking mental ability in childhood. In one study, six-year-old children who were given music lessons showed a significant increase in intelligence tests compared with those who took drama lessons or received no extra instruction.

Too stupid to learn

Albert Einstein is recognized as having had one of the greatest intellects on the planet. Yet there was no sign of his genius when he was young. His performance at school was very poor. In fact, his teachers told his parents to take him out of school because he was "too stupid to learn" and it would be a waste of resources to invest time and energy on his education. The school even suggested that his parents find Albert a simple manual labor job as soon as possible. Instead of following the school's advice, Einstein's mother bought him a violin. Albert loved playing the instrument and practiced until he was highly accomplished. Could music have been the key to Einstein's incredible intellect? He certainly thought so, and a friend of his said that Einstein solved many of his most puzzling physics problems and mathematical equations while improvising on the violin.

So, if you've always wanted to learn to play an instrument or take lessons, there is everything to gain and nothing to lose. You can learn to play a musical instrument by yourself with a helpful instruction manual, but nothing beats interaction with a good music teacher. The piano is probably the best instrument for a beginner because, unlike many wind or string instruments, you don't have to practice before you can even play a note on it. Electronic piano keyboards are relatively cheap and portable, so you don't need to invest in a full-size piano. It might be a good idea to borrow one first to see if it is for you.

If you aren't keen on the piano, there are many other instruments to consider, such as the drums or guitar. An advantage of playing a wind instrument, such as the recorder, oboe, or trumpet, is that it also helps you improve breath control and increases oxygen supply to the brain.

Tuning in

Don't worry if you haven't got the time or the inclination to learn a musical instrument. There are plenty of other ways to bring music into your life. For example:

❏ Singing in the shower or car—or anywhere you like—has mood-enhancing qualities. You can often tell that a person is in a good mood if they are humming or singing.

❏ Toning may fine-tune your brain. The word "toning" goes back to the fourteenth century and means to make sounds with elongated vowels for extended periods of time. "Ahhh," "Ooo," "Eee," "Ayyy," "Ohhh," and "Ommm" are examples of toning sounds. Saying, "Ahhh" immediately feels relaxing. "Eee" or "Ayyy" are more stimulating and help with concentration. "Ohhh" or "Ommm" are considered the richest of sounds, and can relax muscle tension. Try toning for five minutes every day for two weeks to see if it helps you.

❏ Humming can make a positive difference, too. Mozart hummed as he composed. Children hum when they are happy. Adults often hum tunes that go through their minds, lifting their spirits and fine-tuning their mind. So why not try humming during the day? As the sound activates your brain, you will feel more alive and your brain will be more tuned in to the moment.

❏ Try moving to the music. Your brain and body love rhythm. Dancing to your favorite music at home or at a disco, club, or dance class can be highly invigorating physically, emotionally, and mentally.

❏ Finally, just enjoy listening to a lot of great music. From country to jazz, or from rock to classical, music is one of the true joys of life. Bear in mind, though, that certain music, such as heavy metal, especially if it is played loud, can have a negative effect on the mind, whereas beautiful, soothing, melodic music is more likely to make a positive difference to your brain.

Whether you believe in the Mozart effect or not, it's impossible to deny the incredible power of music. Music can speed you up and slow you down. Music can make you laugh and make you smile. Music can inspire and music can stimulate. In all these different ways it is bound to have some beneficial effect on the brain.

Step 4
DEEP INTO SLEEP

adequate sleep is crucial to proper brain function—no less so than air, water, and food. Sleep is needed for the repair and maintenance of the brain and for storing the memories and skills we have acquired during the day. So a chronic lack of sleep is highly damaging. Planning, problem solving, learning, concentration, creativity, working memory, and alertness are all affected by lack of sleep, and exam scores plunge. You can't learn or concentrate well if you are tired. Insomniacs report memory difficulties, poor performance at school or work, problems concentrating,

Sleep on it

When you are asleep, your brain processes new memories, practices new skills—and even solves problems. It seems that sleep somehow allows your brain to juggle stored information to produce flashes of creative insight. Paul McCartney heard a haunting melody in one of his dreams, and once he had confirmed that none of his fellow Beatles had ever heard it before, he wrote it down. It became the tune for his famous song "Yesterday." So, if you want to have a "Eureka!" moment, stop racking your brain and get your head down!

and have twice as many fatigue-related car accidents as good sleepers. In short, a good night's sleep is essential for healthy brain function.

Time for bed

The body and brain feel and work so much better after a good night's sleep. Sleep is not merely down time between episodes of being alive. We spend up to a third of our lives asleep, so it's essential for our general health and well-being. There is an overwhelming body of evidence to suggest that lack of sleep may be related to obesity, diabetes, and many other illnesses, as well as to accidents, errors, and generally poor performance.

Those who suffer from insomnia find it difficult to get all the sleep they want, no matter how hard they try. But some people choose to cut their sleep time on a regular basis, perhaps by staying up watching a late-night film, chatting with friends, or going out clubbing every night. When you are young, especially, it is easy to think that you can make up the sleep you have lost by having an occasional lie-in. But regular sleep deprivation has a cumulative effect on the brain that is not easily reversed.

You may feel you have to cut back on sleep, for example, so that you can make an early start at work. But that isn't the way to increase your productivity. In fact, it has the opposite effect. So make time for rest and recovery. Getting a good night's sleep is one of the best ways to boost your brain power.

How much sleep do I need?

Everyone has different sleep needs. Your greatest requirement for sleep is when you are young. Babies and infants spend much of their time asleep. Children and adolescents usually need eight or more hours a night. But that need steadily decreases as you get older. Until recently, eight hours' sleep a night was regarded as the ideal requirement for all adults. But now sleep experts say that quality—not quantity—is the key when it comes to night-time rest and recuperation. Seven hours a night seems to be the most beneficial, but six hours of good quality sleep is far better than a restless eight. If any of the descriptions on the list below applies to you, you are probably not getting enough quality sleep.

❏ You yawn a lot.
❏ You fall asleep during the day.
❏ You lack energy.
❏ You need caffeine and other stimulants to get you through the day.
❏ You have dark circles under your eyes.
❏ You find it difficult to wake up in the morning.
❏ You find it hard to concentrate on work or school.
❏ You get irritable for no reason.

How to get a good night's sleep

The following tips can help prepare your body so that sleep will come more easily, is less likely to be interrupted, and will be more beneficial for your brain.

❑ Boost your levels of serotonin (the hormone that promotes good sleep) and vitamin B$_6$ by eating lean meat, fish, eggs, soy products, spinach, lentils, carrots, sweet potatoes, and low-fat cheese.

❑ Drink a glass of warm milk (best to make it skim) before you sleep to relax yourself.

❑ Get plenty of exposure to daylight. Light is necessary for serotonin production, so try to get out in the open air every day.

❑ Eat foods that are rich in calcium, magnesium, and silicon, as they can induce a calming state of mind. Good sources of these minerals include broccoli, parsley, leeks, spinach, almonds, sesame seeds, peas, beans, lentils, brown rice, bananas, and raisins.

❑ Establish good sleeping habits. That means going to bed at the same time each night and—even more important—getting up at the same time each morning. Set your alarm for the same time every day, including weekends, and avoid sleeping late, which can disrupt your body clock and make it more difficult to get to sleep.

Sound sleep strategies

❑ Develop a relaxation routine that helps you wind down in the hour or so before you go to bed. For example, take a warm bath, perhaps adding some relaxing aromatherapy oils, such as lavender or bergamot, or try relaxation techniques such as meditation or yoga (see pages 15 and 27). Perhaps you'd prefer to do some gentle stretches, make love, write letters, or update your diary, have a gentle massage, drink some chamomile tea, or sprinkle a few drops of calming lavender essential oil on your pillow—anything that makes you feel relaxed.

❑ Try not to overstimulate your body and mind just before bedtime. For example, avoid energetic exercise, or exciting books or television shows just before bedtime. (Ideally, choose a dull book for your bedtime reading so there is no temptation to stay awake to finish it!)

❑ If you find you can't sleep, don't stay in bed fretting. Get up and read a book, write a letter, or do something tedious like ironing. Then when you feel really sleepy, go back to bed.

❑ Avoid eating a heavy meal before bedtime. Your body needs to rest, not digest, so ideally finish your main meal before 8 p.m.

❑ Avoid stimulants such as caffeine and excess alcohol at least four hours before you go to bed, as both cause insomnia and disturbed sleep patterns.

❑ Make sure your sleeping conditions are conducive to

a good night's rest. If your mattress is uncomfortable, it is worthwhile investing in a new, good-quality one. Try to block out as much noise as possible and make sure the room is well ventilated and cool—around 60°F is ideal.

❑ Keep your curtains closed to block out as much light as you can. The hormone melatonin, which is important for regulating your sleep cycle, is synthesized from serotonin while you sleep. But this process can be inhibited if there is too much light in the room.

❑ Try to be in bed before midnight, if possible— or sooner if you have to make an early start in the morning—so that you get at least seven hours' sleep and awake feeling refreshed.

❑ If you feel like taking a nap during the day, around 15 to 25 minutes is the optimum time to beat fatigue and boost concentration. Any longer than that and you may find it difficult to go to sleep at bedtime.

❑ An hour or two before you go to bed, write a to-do list for the following day and then set your clothes out for the morning. Knowing that you have sorted out your plans for the day ahead means you can put it out of your mind and relax.

❑ Stimulate your brain during the day with plenty of mental activity so that you feel sleepy when you go to bed. Lack of mental stimulation during the day can keep you awake.

If you still find it hard to get quality sleep, try not to get anxious or depressed. If you worry about not getting enough sleep, you are more likely to feel stressed, and that can make it even more difficult to get to sleep. It is not harmful to miss one night's sleep, and you are more likely to sleep soundly the next night, especially if you're eating healthily, getting plenty of exercise, and stimulating your mind (by reading this book!).

Sleep strategies for shift workers and those with an unusual schedule

The first rule of good sleep for those with challenging hours, such as shift workers and new moms, is to keep a regular bed schedule. You need to consider your day sleep the same way someone else considers their night sleep. Diet and exercise advice remains the same. Naps can be lifesavers, but if you overdo them, it may be tough to nod off during normal sleeping hours. And you don't want to nap for more than 30 minutes or so at a stretch.

If you are a shift worker, you tend to be bombarded by things that night sleepers aren't as concerned with: phone calls, lights, the doorbell, etc. So if you work nights, silence the phone during the day if that's practical. Keep the bedroom dark with heavy drapes or wear eyeshades. Talk to family members about the importance of your sleep, and stress that you don't want to be woken up during the day. Keeping your sleeping environment free of sensory input is important. Don't try to totally reverse your schedule on the weekend either, as this will confuse your body clock. You can afford to be more flexible, but try to mimic your workday hours as much as possible.

Step 5
LET'S GET PHYSICAL

It is well known that physical exercise is great for your appearance and your health. It strengthens your heart, lungs, bones, and muscles and can help ward off a host of evils, including obesity, type 2 diabetes, heart disease, and stroke. But what many people don't know is that physical exercise can also boost your brain power. Keeping fit is vital for your brain, as it improves blood flow to your brain cells, increasing the supply of oxygen, glucose energy, and other nutrients to keep it functioning efficiently.

Any physical activity that raises the heart and breathing rate is beneficial. Playing sports, cycling, swimming, doing the household chores, walking briskly, climbing stairs instead of using an elevator, mowing the lawn on a regular basis, will help keep you both physically and mentally fit.

It's never too late to adopt a simple exercise program. Walking at a steady pace for half an hour three times a week can improve brain function at any age. Even gentle exercise, such as yoga, can do wonders for your brain.

Brain-saving exercise prescription

Your exercise routine will depend on your general health. If you haven't exercised for a while, are over 40, have high blood pressure, are overweight, pregnant, or suffering from arthritis, diabetes, or other long-term medical conditions, the first step is to ask your doctor for a checkup.

When you begin your exercise program, start gently and build up steadily as your body adapts. Avoid high-intensity exercise and aim for a moderate level that you can sustain for at least 15 minutes at a time. You may experience a little discomfort or even mild aching at first, but this should soon pass. If you feel more severe muscle ache, it means you are exercising at too intense a level and you should ease off next time. If you experience sharp pain, fainting, dizziness, shortness of breath, or nausea, stop at once.

Wear loose, comfortable clothing and make sure you wear the correct shoes for the activities you plan to do. General-purpose sneakers (such as cross trainers) are ideal for the gym or jogging, and sturdy shoes are best for walking. Drink water before, during, and after your workout, even if you don't feel thirsty (small, regular drinks are best), and have light snacks on hand if you get a sudden dip in energy. Finally, pay attention to your breathing when you're exercising. You should breathe deeply—in through your nose and out through your mouth.

To improve your health, mental functioning, and general quality of life, you should aim to work up to at least 30 minutes of physical activity per day, especially if you have been relatively inactive. Around three times per week, aim to exercise aerobically for the full 30 minutes. At other times, the 30 minutes can be spread out throughout the day and include simple activities such as climbing stairs or doing housework.

Any activity counts as long as it adds up to at least 30 minutes a day most days of the week. If you don't think you're getting your 30 minutes, find other ways to achieve it. Walk to the store more often, get off the bus one or two stops earlier, take the stairs instead of the elevator, carry your groceries home, and wash your car by hand.

Picking up the pace

If you are already getting 30 minutes of exercise a day, you may want to pick up the pace a little and extend your aerobic exercise sessions to pump more oxygen to your ever-hungry brain. Aerobic exercise is any moderate exercise that can be sustained for at least 30 minutes, increases your heart and breathing rate, and leaves you slightly sweaty. Ideally, you should exercise for 20 to 60 minutes, three to five times a week, but if it's all new to you, start with 10 minutes three times a week and build from there.

A good exercise prescription that you can repeat daily, every other day, or three times a week, starts with 5 to 10 minutes of gentle warm-up exercises to increase your heart rate gently. This is followed by moderate-paced aerobic exercise that elevates your heart rate for 20 to 30 minutes. You should feel slightly out of breath but not so much that you can't carry on a conversation. A five-minute cool down period of gentle exercises—like the warm-up—should follow your aerobic workout.

Brisk walking is an ideal form of aerobic exercise, but you may prefer jogging, cycling, an exercise class, or swimming. Whatever you decide, make sure you enjoy it. It doesn't have to be a traditional exercise or class—if dancing, hiking, horseback riding, or boxing are things you enjoy, make them part of your exercise routine.

In addition to your aerobic exercise, it is a good idea to do some gentle stretching every day and include weight-bearing activities two or three times a week. The fitness instructor at your local gym or sports center can advise you on a suitable exercise program, or you could get hold of a good exercise instruction manual, video, or DVD.

You might also ask a partner or friend to exercise with you! You can motivate each other, and it's tougher to break a commitment to exercise if you're with someone else. Or why not persuade friends, neighbors, and family members to get the exercise bug as well and form your

---

The brain-enhancing benefits of exercise

❏ *Improves muscle coordination.*

❏ *Boosts the flow of oxygen, glucose, and other nutrients to the brain.*

❏ *Releases endorphins—"feel-good chemicals"—into the bloodstream (the runner's "high") and combats anxiety, stress, and depression.*

❏ *Exercising to music stimulates the mind at the same time.*

own keep fit class? Working together makes exercising more fun and you can all motivate each other.

Strengthen your motivation

You may find it hard to motivate yourself to exercise on a daily or regular basis, but consider that just 15 to 30 minutes of walking a day can keep you healthy, slim, and happy and significantly boost your brain power.

Physical and mental exercise go hand in hand, so pick an activity you enjoy, and have fun getting physical. If you start a regular exercise program that you enjoy, your body and your brain will thank you. Aerobic exercise improves your mood, boosts the flow of nutrients, and prevents stroke, and there have been studies to show that the brain works more efficiently when exercising, so it is a good time for learning something new.

❏ Take up racquet sports or even skipping rope to improve hand–eye coordination.

❏ Use your exercise time to expand your mind. For example, listen to a personal stereo to learn a language or an audio book or music you wouldn't normally choose, such as classical, folk, or jazz.

❏ When using an exercise bicycle or treadmill, take something to read or study as you work out.

❏ Find an activity that can exercise your mind as well as your body, such as visiting local history sites, bird watching, amateur archeology, and so on.

Step 6
PAY ATTENTION PLEASE

You can be clever, creative, and well-informed, but none of this matters if your mind isn't focused on the task at hand. If you find it hard to concentrate and your thoughts are scattered, it can affect your brain power. Concentration is absolutely crucial for intelligence because if you can't focus, you can't learn. Fortunately, there are easy ways to improve your concentration.

Know your enemy Once you have identified obvious distractions such as noise and interruptions, try to cut down on them. It's a good idea to avoid working near potential diversions, such as the humming noise of a fridge.

Take regular breaks It is important to take a break before you feel tired and lose your concentration completely. Regular breaks—at least once an hour, if not more often—help to sustain your concentration. Alternatively, you can try working for shorter periods of time, such as 20 minutes, and have more frequent but shorter breaks.

Oxygenate Avoid sitting or standing still for long periods. When you take a break, try walking around and doing some light stretching for a few minutes. Take some deep breaths to improve the flow of oxygen to your brain. This will also help to release tension in your body and so ease physical and mental stress.

Rest your eyes If you have been working at a computer or reading a document or book, relax your eyes by looking out of the window and focusing on something in the distance.

Manage your stress levels Aggravating problems and disputes at home or at work can increase stress and have a damaging effect on your brain, especially its ability to concentrate, remember, and learn. The following techniques can help.

Stress management techniques

❏ *Deal with everyday stresses, such as sitting in heavy traffic, deadlines at work, or screaming kids, with simple relaxation techniques—tensing your muscles and relaxing them or deep breathing to a count of 10. Other techniques for relieving short-term stress include talking with friends, drinking calming herbal teas such as chamomile, having a good laugh, writing in a journal, listening to relaxing music, and having a long soak in a warm bath. Sometimes it helps to shout, scream, or punch a cushion to release tension. Exercise is also a great way to reduce stress and boost your energy. (Eating well and taking a daily multivitamin and mineral is a stress buster, too.)*

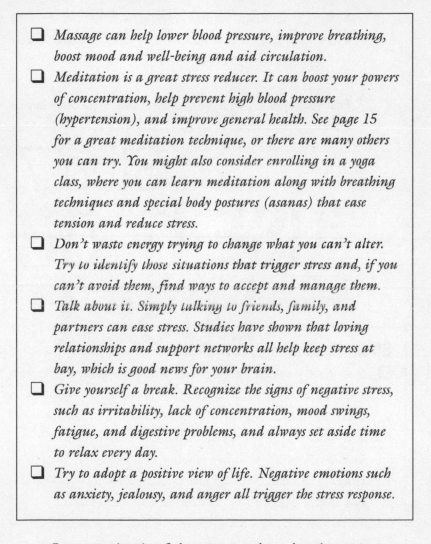

- ❏ *Massage can help lower blood pressure, improve breathing, boost mood and well-being and aid circulation.*
- ❏ *Meditation is a great stress reducer. It can boost your powers of concentration, help prevent high blood pressure (hypertension), and improve general health. See page 15 for a great meditation technique, or there are many others you can try. You might also consider enrolling in a yoga class, where you can learn meditation along with breathing techniques and special body postures (asanas) that ease tension and reduce stress.*
- ❏ *Don't waste energy trying to change what you can't alter. Try to identify those situations that trigger stress and, if you can't avoid them, find ways to accept and manage them.*
- ❏ *Talk about it. Simply talking to friends, family, and partners can ease stress. Studies have shown that loving relationships and support networks all help keep stress at bay, which is good news for your brain.*
- ❏ *Give yourself a break. Recognize the signs of negative stress, such as irritability, lack of concentration, mood swings, fatigue, and digestive problems, and always set aside time to relax every day.*
- ❏ *Try to adopt a positive view of life. Negative emotions such as anxiety, jealousy, and anger all trigger the stress response.*

Concentration is of the utmost value when it comes to learning something new. Try not to become discouraged if you are unable to hold your thoughts on a subject for very long at first. If you practice the techniques in this chapter, your attention span will improve.

Step 7
USE IT OR LOSE IT

there is no doubt that genes, health, and education have a lot to do with determining intelligence—but so does continued mental exercise. Chronological age is not an excuse for mental decline. Your brain is dynamically changing and growing throughout your life and is capable of learning at any time. Mental exercise generates growth in your brain cells. In other words, the more you think, the better your brain works, regardless of your age.

Top mind-saving tips

Practice your powers of observation There are many things in our everyday lives that we don't really register or cannot recall. For example, can you remember whose picture is on a $5 or $20 bill or the exact traffic light sequence? To exercise your powers of observation, get into the habit of using them and observe the little details in your daily life.

Experiment with fragrances Certain aromas, such as peppermint, lemon, vanilla, and lily-of-the-valley, are known to have a stimulating effect on the mind and can improve your attention span, as well as enhance memory.

Keep a diary By recalling what has happened during the day you are helping to exercise your memory. It's also a great emotional release. Writing letters, stories, poetry, or your family history can also help to strengthen memory links.

Learn a new language Most towns have a college or evening class where you can learn a new language. Or you can buy audio tapes and CDs and learn at your own pace. A new language will also enhance your verbal skills, and broaden your mind by introducing you to a new culture.

Expand your vocabulary Adding new words to your vocabulary is a fantastic brain-building exercise. You will enhance your memory, speech, and writing centers and benefit your cognitive abilities. Set yourself a program of learning a new word every day and try to incorporate those new words into everyday speech and writing.

Limit TV time and read instead Some television programs are both entertaining and informative, but much of it is just mental wallpaper that puts your brain into neutral. In fact, studies show that your brain is more active when staring at a blank wall than watching television. Reading not only stimulates your imagination; it also strengthens the language areas and engages both sides of your brain at the same time. For maximum benefit, pause from time to time to think back over what you have read. This will help to fix it in your memory.

Explore the World Wide Web The Internet is a fantastic information resource, giving you access to a world of information, and by following the screen directions and manipulating the mouse you are boosting your reaction times and enhancing hand–eye coordination at the same time.

Play games All games involve challenge, interest, and fun. Bridge and chess are excellent because they require memory and judgment. Crossword puzzles and jigsaws are also great for word recall and spatial judgments. Working with modelling clay or Play-Doh helps develop improved spatial awareness and imagination, as well as mental agility and hand–eye coordination.

Use the other hand This is another version of the exercise you met in Part One that can help strengthen existing neural connections and create new ones. Use the hand you normally do not use to write, control the computer mouse, or turn the page. What do you notice? Is it harder to be precise and accurate? Do you feel the way you did when you were first learning to tie your shoelaces? If you are feeling uncomfortable and awkward, don't worry—this is a good sign. It shows your brain is learning new skills.

Learn a new skill Challenge your brain with new and novel tasks. Here are some suggestions, but you will have many others. Always choose something that appeals to you:

square dancing, chess, tai chi, yoga, sculpture, lace making. Learning or doing something new enhances your skills and knowledge and gives you a feeling of mastery and self-confidence to continue to build your brain power.

Break old habits Changing routines and habits or replacing them with something new increases mental alertness. For example, go to work via a new route. Try shopping at a new grocery store. Drink from a different mug at coffee time. Sit at a different place at the table. Regard your brain as a muscle, and look for new opportunities to flex it. Anything that stimulates your brain to think in a new way is ideal.

Reprogram your mind If you always put yourself down by thinking that, for example, you are too stupid to learn new information or skills, it won't be long before you become reluctant to try anything new. Starting today, stop and reflect whenever you are about to say something negative about yourself and replace it with something positive. For example, swap "I'm stupid" with "I'm learning something new." Replace "I'm always making mistakes" with "I am learning from my mistakes." Switch from "I can't understand that" to "I will soon learn." No matter how unsure you feel right now, start adopting a more positive attitude and you'll soon begin to believe it. Reprogram your mind with positive thoughts and you'll feel happier—and smarter.

Time to wake your mind up

If you want to improve your mind, you need to keep
using it. Keep thinking and working that mental muscle
with enjoyable and challenging tasks. The exercises in this
book are all designed to flex your "mental muscles,"
stretch your mind, and keep your brain alive. What you
do with your brain—how much you challenge and push
it to achieve its full potential—well, that's up to you. Just
remember one thing—with a brain as flexible as yours,
the possibilities are limitless!

ANSWERS

Exercise 4

Line 1: 8 pairs, line 2: 7 pairs, line 3: 7 pairs.

Exercise 22 (task 1)

Wyoming is a state. The others are all cities.

Dandelion is the only plant in the list that is not also a girls' name.

Impatiens is the only flower in the list that is not perennial.

F is the only consonant. The others are vowels.

Acre is a measure of area. All the others measure length.

A barometer measures air pressure. All the others measure time.

Ice hockey is played with a puck. All the others are played with a ball.

All except the novel are reference books.

Exercise 22 (task 2)

T for Tuesday: the letters are the first letters of the days of the week.

Exercise 23

They are all girls' names: AMY, KATE, ALICE, CATHY, MARY.

Exercise 24 (task 1)

Make a square that has three coins on each side then place the remaining four coins on top of each of the four corner coin squares.

Exercise 24 (task 2)

2	9	4
7	5	3
6	1	8

Exercise 24 (task 3)

The solution is to construct one triangle flat on the table and then to build a pyramid of matches on top.

Exercise 25

26 and 6, 3 miles, 45, 140 pounds, 43.

Exercise 26 (task 1)

Sock. A letter is enclosed in an envelope and a foot is enclosed in a sock.

You can't marry someone if you are dead!

You can't take pictures with a hair curler—you need a camera!

Natural causes of course!

13. She could possibly take out six black left-hand gloves and then six brown left-hand gloves. The next one would have to be either the black or brown right-hand match.

Exercise 26 (task 2)

The man is of such small stature that he cannot reach the button for the tenth floor. When he is not alone, the other person in the elevator pushes button 10 for him. When it's raining, the man has an umbrella he can use to extend his reach.

Exercise 27

The surgeon is the boy's mother.

The object she throws is a boomerang. It flies out, loops around, comes back, and hits her on the head.

Time.

He was a priest.

Exercise 28 (task 1)

This solution contains six signs: 12+3–4+5+67+8+9=100. Can you find another solution that uses only three signs?

Exercise 28 (task 2)

They were grandmother, mother, and daughter. They cut the pizza into six and ate two pieces each.

Exercise 29 (task 1)

Break your assumption that lines may not extend beyond the imaginary square and you will solve this puzzle more easily.

Exercise 29 (task 2)

They all have a past tense that rhymes.

Exercise 29 (task 3)

A coffin, of course.

Exercise 30

Mother	Child	Age
Jane	Charlie	3
Teresa	Daniel	4
Laura	Brian	2
Sarah	Anne	1

Exercise 31

The Ss below all represent how the statues should be placed in the room:

```
-----------------------------------
S        S     S

S                       S

S                       S

         S     S         S
-----------------------------------
```

Exercise 41

Read each quote backward!

1) In this world nothing can be said to be certain, except death and taxes.—Benjamin Franklin
2) Three may keep a secret, if two of them are dead. —Benjamin Franklin
3) It is better to offer no excuse than a bad one. —George Washington

Exercise 83

6	4	5	7	9	2	1	8	3
8	7	2	1	4	3	5	9	6
3	1	9	5	8	6	2	4	7
2	3	1	8	5	9	6	7	4
4	8	7	6	2	1	3	5	9
5	9	6	4	3	7	8	1	2
9	6	8	3	7	5	4	2	1
7	5	3	2	1	4	9	6	8
1	2	4	9	6	8	7	3	5

Exercise 88

SMILE, stile, stale, stare, stars, sears, TEARS

NAIL, fail, fall, fill, FILE

GIVE, live, like, lake, TAKE

NAVY, nave, name, dame, dams, dims, aims, arms, ARMY

Exercise 90

1) No conclusion. The dancing rugby players may or may not be ice skaters. It's impossible to tell.
2) Some people we trust are liars.
3) Some successful businesspeople are not young, or All young businesspeople are not successful.

Exercise 91

A sister and a brother, both married. One has a daughter and the other has a son.

About the Author

Carol Vorderman is Britain's leading female television host. For twenty-five years she has been known as the "Numbers Queen" on the hit U.K. quiz show *Countdown,* where she performs mental arithmetic at lightning speed. Carol is an international Sudoku expert whose Sudoku puzzle books have sold millions of copies worldwide. She holds a degree from Cambridge and is a member of MENSA, with an IQ of 154. She lives in London.